More Praise for
10 Steps to Successful Bu

"Jack Appleman's *10 Steps to Successf* perfectly aligned with today's business is an excellent resource, and an enormously helpful business writing guide."

—Courtland L. Hines
Senior Manager, Johnson & Johnson

"Jack Appleman offers a time-tested, user-friendly approach that helps executives who don't necessarily write for a living communicate more effectively and powerfully, even in an age where tweets pass for major pronouncements."

—Sam Friedman
Insurance Research Leader
Deloitte Center for Financial Services

"Appleman's first edition is required reading for my graduate students because it provides outstanding guidance for writing clearly and concisely. The new edition is even better, with sections on social media, email communication, and mobile writing. This book has helped my students and coaching clients land jobs and advance in their careers."

—Nancy Ancowitz
Presentation and Career Coach
Adjunct Faculty, New York University

"More clarity, less verbiage. That's the central message Jack Appleman preaches, and every professional needs to heed it. This book shows why clear communication is not a luxury—it's a strategic advantage."

—Steve Woodruff
President, Impactiviti

"Good writing goes unnoticed; poor writing always gets noticed. Jack provides an excellent primer on key writing skills and techniques from which all writers can benefit. His 10-step approach is easy to follow, yet comprehensive and powerful. All corporate professionals should make this book a must read."

—Tony Irace
Learning and Development Executive, ADP

"As a business editor and reporter, I'm grateful to have picked up *10 Steps to Successful Business Writing*. The tips for social media and other forms of electronic writing are invaluable as business news competition from various social media platforms and websites intensifies on a daily basis."

—Anthony Birritteri
Editor-in-Chief, New Jersey Business Magazine

"In this book, Jack Appleman doesn't just show us the tricks of the trade; he gives us the keys to the kingdom. If you take his word and follow his lessons, you will be doing yourself a great professional service—and you will write better."

—Thom Gencarelli
Professor and Chair of Communication,
Manhattan College

"The ability to recognize and seize opportunities to train our employees is key. In *10 Steps to Successful Business Writing*, Jack Appleman shows how important it is to continuously develop your skills as business writing evolves with your environment."

—Lindsay Gaal
Director, Human Resources, Friedman

"As you'd expect in a book about clear writing, Jack Appleman's pointers for better communication are easy to understand and simple to put into practice. His guidance on tone is particularly important in today's business environment, where so much writing is delivered electronically. Highly recommended for people who want to get their message across and boost productivity at work."

—Elizabeth Harrin
Content Strategist and Blogger, GirlsGuideToPM.com

"Jack Appleman's writing methods have helped my business with email composition. They are concise and effective—converting prospects into loyal clients!"

—Michael Cicchine
Founder, Mindbrand

"This book provides invaluable insights and advice on how to master business writing in the digital era. Jack Appleman builds on his earlier edition to show how the fundamentals of effective writing need to be adapted to the digital and social media world. It's a brilliant must-read for business writers at every level."

—Patrick Ford
Worldwide Vice Chairman and Chief Client Officer,
Burson-Marsteller

10
Steps to
Successful

Business Writing

Jack E. Appleman

2nd Edition

atd
PRESS

ATD Press is an internationally renowned source of insightful and practical information on talent development, training, and professional development.

ATD Press
1640 King Street
Alexandria, VA 22314 USA

Ordering information: Books published by ATD Press can be purchased by visiting ATD's website at www.td.org/books or by calling 800.628.2783 or 703.683.8100.

Library of Congress Control Number: 2017954650

ISBN-10: 1-947308-30-0
ISBN-13: 978-1-947308-30-5
e-ISBN: 978-1-947308-31-2

ATD Press Editorial Staff
Director: Kristine Luecker
Manager: Melissa Jones
Community of Practice Manager, Management: Ryan Changcoco
Developmental Editor: Jack Harlow
Cover Design: Derek Thornton, Faceout Studio
Text Design: Iris Sanchez

Printed by Versa Press Inc., East Peoria, IL

CONTENTS

Preface

"Nobody can write anymore!" That's all I hear from executives, human resource managers, learning and development specialists, and others when I explain my profession as a corporate writing instructor and coach. And they're right, based on many studies on the impact of poor writing in the workplace. According to the *Los Angeles Business Journal,* "Billions of dollars in lost productivity can be traced to employees who are not capable of writing clearly and concisely" (Killeen 2013).

Today, the need for effective business writing has never been greater. With the rising number of communication channels—social media, instant messaging, and whatever else is next—and the accelerating pace of business interaction, we're writing more than ever. And what we say and how we say it can dramatically affect our careers and the success of organizations in which we work.

Whether it's providing clear directions to direct reports, conveying bad news to a client, or posting a meaningful comment on social media, your writing needs to be concise, explicit, relevant, professional, well organized, and free of grammatical errors. Plus, in many cases, your text must be captivating enough to break through the clutter and grab readers' attention.

The good news is that business writing is a learned skill based on fundamental principles of communication. It doesn't matter how extensive your vocabulary is or what grades you received in high school or college English. If you can tap your natural ability to express your thoughts, first learned as a child, you can become an effective writer. This is the essence of business writing: Say it as simply as possible so the reader understands and takes the desired action. As you read the techniques, tools, and exercises in *10 Steps to Successful Business Writing,* remember this simple—and powerful—statement.

Why a Second Edition?

Have the skills for successful business writing changed since the first edition was published in 2008? Not really; they've remained virtually identical for the past 75 years or more. But a few aspects have changed. The speed of business communication has accelerated, spurring a greater need for concise, clear, and compelling text—which must be written faster than ever. That puts added pressure on you to quickly crank out messages that achieve the desired results and demands an important talent: critical thinking on the go.

Moreover, the digital era seems to have spawned an attention deficit disorder epidemic. Fewer people have the patience to read one paragraph after another. Everyone wants information in bite-sized chunks. So you need to master subject lines, titles, subheads, and bulleted text. Otherwise, your readers won't pay attention to your message.

Today, everyone wants to be "social," in their personal lives and in their work environments. Some organizations expect their employees to participate regularly in traditional social media forums, like LinkedIn and their social enterprise networks, to support various initiatives. That means tough decisions: How do you start? Should you be edgy? How will audiences react to you? It goes back to critical thinking on the go.

Maybe the best reason for a second edition is all of you. Since the first edition came out in 2008, I've received so many valuable insights from readers; participants in my corporate writing workshops, coaching sessions, and college classes; and colleagues, friends, and family members. You've shared your toughest writing challenges, your most important takeaways from the book, and additional areas to address in this new edition.

So here are your 10 steps with the changes from the first edition:

- **Step 1: Get Started Easily and Naturally** updates the old Step 2 (Know Where You're Taking Your Readers).
- **Step 2: Be Concise, Explicit, and Clear** updates the old Step 3 (Be Explicit, Clear, and Concise).
- **Step 3: Write With Style and Rhythm** updates the old Step 5 (Write With Rhythm to Hold Your Readers).
- **Step 4: Organize to Promote Understanding** updates the old Step 6 (Organize to Help Your Readers Understand).
- **Step 5: Persuade Readers to Take Your Desired Action** updates the old Step 4 (Grab Your Readers' Attention).
- **Step 6: Choose the Right Tone** updates the old Step 7 (Choose a Tone That Produces Good Results).
- **Step 7: Put Your Best Grammar on the Page** updates the old Step 8 (Put Your Best Grammar on the Page).
- **Step 8: Edit and Proofread Effectively** updates the old Step 9 (Edit, Rewrite, and Refine).
- **Step 9: Master Emails and Electronic Communication** is a new step.
- **Step 10: Apply Writing Skills to Social Media Copy** is a new step.
- **Appendix A: Drive Organizational and Personal Success With Better Writing** updates the old appendix (Steps to Improve Workers' Writing Skills).
- **Appendix B: Master the Text You Write Most Often** updates the old Step 10 (Master the Documents You Use Most Often).
- **Appendix C: Commonly Misused Words and Phrases** updates a tool in the old Step 8 (Put Your Best Grammar on the Page).

Acknowledgments

For me, taking on a major creative endeavor like writing a book is much easier with the support of people who care about me. A big thanks to Rosa, my wife; my younger daughter, Sarah; my older daughter, Gail, and her husband, Grayson; my granddaughter, Norah; and my mother-in-law, Lupe. Knowing that you were all behind me made all the difference in the world.

Writing a book is a team effort. And I couldn't have done it without the shrewd advice and continual support I received from my team at ATD: Jack Harlow, Melissa Jones, Caroline Coppel, Hannah Sternberg, Ryan Changcoco, and Kristine Luecker. You made this challenging process more manageable—and a lot more fun!

Finally, I need to thank an individual no longer with us, Christine Cotting, my editor (from ATD) for the first edition of the book. With patience, compassion, and a zeal for excellence, she coached me through each step, explaining the nuances of writing effective copy. Christine, you're sorely missed by me as well as countless authors, former colleagues, and others lucky enough to have known you.

Introduction

I'm frequently asked to identify the single most important quality for good business writing. My answer is always the same: simplicity. It's what readers crave and what will get you the desired results. Yet it can be elusive.

If your text lacks simplicity, you may be overcomplicating your message, perhaps subconsciously. You may be trying to dazzle your reader with million-dollar words. Or you may be including superfluous information in an attempt to be comprehensive. Always go back to the essence of business writing—getting the reader to understand your message as quickly as possible.

Consider these advertising examples that illustrate the power of simplicity:

> Around 1990, a major technology company aired a television commercial for its software consulting services that went something like this: One man (we'll call him Bob) is rattling off complex technical jargon to explain to a colleague (let's call him Dave) why his firm should invest in a particular software application. Frustrated with this over-the-top language, Dave implores Bob to cut the technobabble and explain the purchase rationale in a way that management could understand. Bob pauses, reconsiders his initial choice of words, and says: "For every buck we invest, we'll get back two." So simple, so concise, so powerful!

Now, consider three iconic advertising slogans:

> Nike: "Just do it."
> Subway: "Eat fresh."
> BMW: "The ultimate driving machine."

These companies recognize that the window in which to hook their audience is limited, whether at the end of a 30-second commercial or on a highway billboard. Competing for attention against other brands, not to mention countless other distractions, advertisers know that simplicity is the best way to get people's attention and drive them to action.

But simplicity isn't always easy to achieve—we often make it hard on ourselves by losing touch with the core message. Take a look at these notifications I've come across while navigating my computer:

- "Avsynmgr has caused an error in MCSCAN32DLL. The application will close." *Oh, I get it. I knew I should have paid more attention to my Avsynmgr.*
- "The instruction at OxSad715131 referenced memory at Ox0000019. The memory could not be found." *I knew it. I should've referenced that memory at Ox0000019 like I usually do.*
- "The application Windows Genuine Advantage Notification has changed since you first gave it access to the Internet. Do you still want to let it access the Internet?" *I want to access the Internet and don't care if Windows Genuine Advantage Notification (whatever that is) can access it.*

If you're an information technology specialist, these messages may be perfectly clear to you—but not to me or the majority of laypeople who depend on computers and mobile devices. The software developers lost the essence of the message they were trying to convey with these alerts, and as a result, have hindered the users' comprehension of what action they need to take. The good news is that over the past few years, technology and software companies have started to recognize that we need plain instructions—with no chance for misunderstanding. Thank you, Microsoft, for your brilliantly direct messages, such as, "Please do not turn off your computer when configuring Windows and installing updates." Simplicity is a beautiful thing!

The Demand for Good Writing

Today, working professionals at all levels need to deliver information instantly and accurately to a wide array of discerning readers. Top executives insist that your emails get to the point immediately. Prospective clients need your proposal to explain precisely what separates your firm from competitors. And managers, colleagues, suppliers, and everyone else need text with clear rationale and explicit instructions.

But the quality of business writing continues to fall short of these requirements, based on my experience and observations over the past 20 years. Too many documents, emails, and text messages lack clarity and professionalism and ignore basic grammar rules. Poor writing is an epidemic spreading throughout the workplace. Check out these alarming statistics:

- Bad writing costs American businesses close to $400 billion every year (Bernoff 2016).
- Poor communication (including emails that don't reach their audiences) is responsible for as much 40 percent of the cost of managing all business transactions (DuBay 2008).
- Only 6 to 7 percent of emails receive a response (Mark, Voida, and Cardello 2012).

And to address these deficiencies, U.S. companies spend more than $3.1 billion annually on remedial writing training, including $2.9 million on existing, rather than new, employees (National Commission on Writing and CollegeBoard 2004). This figure has probably risen considerably since the study was published.

Why Don't We Like to Write?

One reason cited for poor workplace writing is that it's one of the least favorite activities for many employees. For some, this aversion goes all the way back to elementary school, when writing was a dreaded assignment. Some teachers, instead of encouraging our creativity and allowing us to experiment with word construction, fixated on correctness—pointing out every last grammar and spelling mistake, slashing handwritten or typed papers with red ink. That's no way to encourage people to write!

Then came high school and college English courses. Remember? Your 1,000-word essay is due tomorrow morning and you're still 300 words short. You crank out some more sentences. You plug in some flowery new vocabulary words—even if you're not sure what they mean—to impress the teacher. So what if you're rephrasing ideas already written? Keep those words coming until you reach that magic 1,000 mark.

What an agonizing way to write! Yet too many working professionals of all ages haven't let go of this "essay syndrome"—piling up words that don't contribute meaning—and their writing suffers. For them, the consequence is far worse than a poor grade: People lose interest and stop reading their text.

I don't mean to disparage English teachers, who play a critical role in teaching us the fundamentals such as grammar, syntax, and vocabulary. As a business writer, you need to master these skills or risk embarrassing yourself before supervisors, clients, colleagues, and other key audiences. Still, I appeal to all teachers, from elementary school through college: Stress clarity and brevity, the qualities your students will need when they write as working professionals.

Effective Writing Can Be Learned

My goal for you and everyone reading this book is to become a more confident writer. Start with the belief that you can significantly improve your writing by learning several easy-to-follow techniques.

One essential strategy is to stop trying to impress readers. You're *not* completing an academic assignment and won't be judged on the breadth of your vocabulary or whether you surpass a minimum number of words. Instead, you're trying to convey your message in a straightforward, concise, and organized manner. Do that and you'll become a successful business writer.

This goal is well within your reach; just follow the steps in this book. And pay more attention to how others write, everyone from authors and journalists to top executives, middle managers, colleagues, and direct reports. As a reader, notice what's clear and what's confusing. Evaluate how effectively the information is presented to you—a process that will help you deliver effective messages to others.

The Payoff of Good Writing

In the corporate world, your documents, emails, and instant messages become your personal brand. Co-workers, clients, suppliers, and others form impressions about you based on your written words, which can convey enthusiasm, intelligence, and empathy, and inspire others to action. These written messages can fuel your ability to be a more effective leader. Here's how:

- As a company head, you can shape the future of your organization.
- As a senior executive, you can clarify complex sales or management strategies.
- As a midlevel manager, you can demonstrate or underscore your leadership abilities to direct reports and supervisors.

Above all, as an employee at any level, well-written text can also show others that:

- You understand all aspects of a situation and can clearly convey their relevance.
- You understand how a problem affects various people a nd departments.
- You can "manage up," which includes helping a supervisor understand an issue and weigh potential solutions.
- You know what steps others should take and why they should take them.

Inside This Book

This book has been designed for people at different levels of writing proficiency, ranging from those looking to polish their superior text to those who struggle to find the right words, including those for whom English is a second language.

If you're looking for a book with extensive discussion on the philosophy of writing, audience analysis, readability matrixes, sentence diagrams, and endless grammar rules, this isn't it. I didn't have the patience to go into such detail—and you probably wouldn't have had the patience to read it. Instead, I developed a short, practical guide with the most important steps for taking your writing to the next level.

The skills are explained through examples, in which you'll see the same message presented two ways, one less polished and one preferred. Then, in the "Your Turn" section at the end of each step, you'll get a chance to complete exercises addressing these concepts. Here's a preview of how examples will be shown:

> **Too Many Words:** Starting next year, our division will sponsor monthly social outings. These will be designed for the purpose of building camaraderie among all personnel, enabling employees to better know their fellow workers.
> **Concise:** Starting next year, our division will sponsor monthly social outings to help build camaraderie among the staff.

Much of the content in the book is based on my 20-plus years as a business writing instructor, writing coach, and professor. Feedback from employees and students I've taught (especially in the 10 years since the first edition was published) helped me identify common challenges and the most desired competencies. Here are your 10 steps to writing effective business text.

Step 1: Get Started Easily and Naturally

Unleash your innate ability to communicate effectively. Break through writer's block by answering a few simple questions that define your message. Then choose a method such as outlining or freewriting, and you're on your way.

Step 2: Be Concise, Explicit, and Clear

Get to the point immediately with clarity and precision. Spare readers the murky swamp of vague terms, jargon, buzzwords, and stuffy phrases.

Step 3: Write With Style and Rhythm

With a professional and down-to-earth style, create a smooth flow of words and sentences. Insert transitions to unify your ideas so readers move easily through your message.

Step 4: Organize to Promote Understanding

Select the organizing method best suited for each document you create. Hold readers' attention so they grasp your points. Start with the bottom line and arrange ideas in a logical order. Use tools such as subheads to separate sections and topic sentences to frame ideas.

Step 5: Persuade Readers to Take Your Desired Action

Push readers' hot buttons, address their WIIFM (what's it in for me?), and overcome their objections to win them over to your side. Strengthen your persuasive emails with active verbs and compelling language.

Step 6: Choose the Right Tone

Compose messages that convey professionalism, respect, and empathy. Avoid hidden insults, and reply civilly to rude emails or text messages. Fit your language and your attitude to each reader's needs.

Step 7: Put Your Best Grammar on the Page

Use your common sense when following grammar rules. Avoid frequently made errors, and learn which old rules can be broken. Don't expect perfection, but ensure that substandard grammar never muddles your message.

Step 8: Edit and Proofread Effectively

Put yourself in your readers' shoes and refine your text until your gut tells you it's ready. Then proofread it for clarity, organization, and mechanics.

Step 9: Master Emails and Electronic Communication

Enhance email efficiency with precise messages and clear next steps, avoiding excessive back-and-forth dialogue. Spur action with explicit subject lines. Practice proper etiquette for email and instant messaging to save time and to come across professionally.

Step 10: Apply Writing Skills to Social Media Copy

Tailor your writing to platforms, such as LinkedIn, Facebook, and Twitter, and to social enterprise networks within your organization. Speak one-on-one to your audience, and stop readers with engaging headlines. Ask intriguing questions, and post thoughtful replies that extend conversations.

Appendix A: Drive Organizational and Personal Success With Better Writing

Determine how the quality of writing affects productivity, profitability, and engagement. Identify employees at all levels who need to upgrade their writing skills. Get management buy-in, and design a sustainable writing training program tailored to participants' needs. And devise a plan to improve your own writing.

Appendix B: Master the Text You Write Most Often

Become adept at writing the kind of text you most frequently compose to save time and get better results. See how the 10 steps apply to a performance review, an audit report, a proposal, an email to irritated customer, presentation slides, a project status report, a press release, and a LinkedIn profile summary.

Appendix C: Commonly Misused Words and Phrases

Make the grammatically correct choice when deciding between more than 25 confusing pairs of words, including aggravate and irritate, comprise and compose, and imply and infer.

Step 1

Get Started Easily and Naturally

Overview

- Answer a few questions to clarify your message.
- Overcome writer's block—write like you speak.
- Jump-start your writing through outlining, freewriting, or a structured process.

The blank screen is staring back at you. How should you start?

Many writers—including journalists, novelists, and bloggers—frequently struggle to figure out what they're going to say and how they're going to say it. If you have a get-started system that works, more power to you. But if you spend too much time looking at a blank page, check out the strategies that follow.

Start With a Few Basic Questions

Begin with what you know. To help define your purpose and message, answer these questions:

1. What is the situation, problem, or issue that is prompting you to write?

2. Who is going to read it?

3. What do your readers need to know?

4. What action do you want your readers to take?

To see how these questions help you begin writing, let's say that your company's travel costs are too high, and your boss, a senior executive, has demanded that expenses be reduced. That's the answer to question one—the problem that prompts you to write. So you need to inform the division heads who report to you that travel costs must be lowered and explain the recommended measures to achieve this goal.

The answer to question two (who are your readers?) is your direct reports. For your readers to act on this request, they need to know several things (question three):

- Travel expenses rose 30 percent—$175,000—this year, compared with the same period last year.
- Your division must lower travel costs by at least $100,000 next year.
- Working with the finance team, we've come up with three steps to achieve this goal:
  - videoconferencing sales meetings every other month
  - booking plane tickets two months ahead of travel to take advantage of lower fares
  - arranging for group rates at mid-range hotels instead of higher-priced properties.

When your readers have grasped that information, you want them to take these steps (question four):

- Let me know by February 1 if you can implement these steps and save $100,000 or more next year.
- Contact me if you have any questions or if you need to schedule a call to discuss the proposal.

By answering these four key questions, you've virtually drafted the entire email. It's not always that easy, especially with complex documents, but answering the questions can often help you get started writing faster.

Write Like You Speak

This might sound counterintuitive. Many people try *not* to write like they talk. They believe that they speak in language that's disjointed and too informal for written business communication. But that's not normally the case. Saying your message out loud can free you to express your thoughts in a clear, uncomplicated manner. In my 20 years of one-on-one writing coaching, this type of conversation keeps repeating itself:

> **Me:** I don't understand what you're trying to say in this paragraph.
> **Individual:** I'm trying to say "this," "this," and "this" (each representing a concept).
> **Me:** Then write "this," "this," and "this"!

Most people find talking easier than writing. And their spoken language is typically more straightforward and concise than their written text. So if you're ever stuck on what to write, think about how you'd say it in an oral conversation. Then move those naturally flowing words from your lips to the keyboard, and make a few edits as needed. This goes back to the essence of business writing—conveying your message as simply as you can.

POINTER

If you're stuck getting started, write the words you'd use in a conversation.

The following example illustrates how writing what you would instinctively say out loud can help overcome writer's block: You're about to start writing an email to your supervisor, summarizing yesterday's meeting about strategies for LX Partners, one of your company's most important clients. No one else from your firm attended the meeting. While staring at the screen, you get a frantic call from your supervisor.

"Listen," he says, "LX Partners wants me to be on a conference call in two minutes and I have no idea what happened at yesterday's meeting. You were there. I need you to tell me—in 60 seconds—what was decided and what the next steps are!"

Talk about being put on the spot. But that's good, because your boss's demand for the bottom-line information in one minute forces you to get to the point and omit the unimportant details.

After a few moments of panic, you intuitively focus on the relevant information you know he wants and reply, "LX Partners has had three system-level security breaches in the past six months. In the meeting, I recommended that LX invest $200,000 on a new software system that would prevent breaches at the application level. This purchase needs to be approved by April 1 to be fully operational by July 1."

The takeaway: If you're forced to be concise, you *will* be concise! So approach every email, text, and document with the same urgency you'd feel if the reader were talking to you on the phone or standing beside your desk impatiently waiting for your spoken answer. In other words, write it like you'd say it!

Develop an Outline for Complex Documents

The traditional outline you learned somewhere between grade school and high school can still work well, especially for longer documents like proposals, procedures, and reports. Start with general categories and then incorporate more specific ones. Example 1-1 shows how an outline could be developed.

Feel free to use roman numerals or any combination of bullets, letters, and numerals that's clear to you. Remember, readers will only see your final document, not all the drafts you use to get there.

EXAMPLE 1-1
OUTLINE OF PLAN TO OUTSOURCE TRAINING

Purpose: Suggest outsourcing time management training

List simple, general categories:

1. Introduction: recommend outsourcing time management training
2. Why we need it
3. Implementing the training
4. Benefits of outsourced versus in-house training
5. Cost
6. Next steps

Expand categories with more details:

- Introduction: recommend outsourcing time management training
- Why we need it
  - Staff works inefficiently
  - Too many projects behind schedule
  - In-house training is not practical
- Implementing the training
  - Suppliers (training firms) that would meet our needs
    - Supplier A: pros and cons
    - Supplier B: pros and cons
    - Supplier C: pros and cons
  - Setting objectives
  - Scheduling
  - Evaluation and follow-up
- Benefits of outsourcing the training
  - Staff working 15 percent more efficiently
  - Better morale
  - Greater productivity
- Cost
  - Facilitation fees
  - Video tutorials
  - Other expenses
- Next steps
  - Management approval
  - Selecting a supplier
  - Scheduling training
  - Developing evaluation method

For more about organizing your text, see Step 4 (Organize to Promote Understanding).

Freewriting: Your Personal Brainstorm

Another method for getting started is called freewriting, because it frees you from all those constraints of writing—spelling, grammar, sentence structure, organization, and your own judgment—that can stifle your ability to crank out the right words. When you freewrite on a topic, you just unleash your thoughts and get them on the screen or on paper as quickly as you can. What you write can be cut, organized, and better expressed later. What matters is that you dump out all your thoughts about the subject—and then feel good because you started.

Here's what freewriting might produce for a blog post on effective customer service over the phone:

POINTER

To freewrite, just write down your thoughts on the topic.

Customer service over the phone stinks in most cases. Companies don't put enough effort to training the reps or they don't teach the right skills. Most people can't stand talking to service reps over the phone. It's so frustrating—I've had to do it and what a waste of time. What kills me is the phoniness of it all. Those reps sound like robots. "Yes, I'll be happy to help you with that," or some other canned response. These reps don't really listen to what you say—they may hear but they don't really listen. And they've got this surly attitude that makes the customer feel like chopped liver.

Be real, be genuine—that's the way to service customers. There's actually a simple step to come across more friendly over the phone and show that you're willing to solve their problem. Smile—yea, just smile! It actually releases endorphins that put you in a better mood. And you know that customers will sense that when they hear your voice. Reps need to ask better questions. If their questions were better, they'd get to the crux of the customer's problem sooner. I couldn't believe when I heard that 84 percent of people said their expectations weren't exceeded in their last customer service interaction. That's from *Harvard Business Review*. Reps should show more empathy and let customers know that they feel the person's frustration.

Poor customer service can be brutal to companies. People stop buying products when service is lousy. I couldn't believe when I read that a lot people who were going to purchase something decided not to because of poor customer service. It was more than half—55 percent—according to American Express. Corporate America isn't doing enough about this—and they're missing a huge opportunity. Effective customer service promotes additional purchases. And here's a hopeful stat: 73 percent of consumers say customer service reps who are friendly (not easy to find!) can make them fall in love with a brand, according to RightNow Technologies. That's huge!

While it's an extremely rough draft, it's a start.

To create order from the chaos of your freewritten document, read it over and pick out the key points you need to communicate to readers. When put into a logical order, these points will form your outline. Using the previous freewritten paragraphs, you might create this outline:

Effective customer service over the phone:

- Poor customer service on the phone: a critical business problem
- Alarming statistics on cost to corporate America:
  - 55 percent of consumers who intended to make a purchase backed out because of poor customer service (American Express)
  - 84 percent of consumers said that their expectations hadn't been exceeded in their last customer service interaction (*Harvard Business Review*)
- Lack of adequate training
- Consumers' most frequent complaints about reps:
  - Phony, canned replies
  - Failure to listen
  - Surly attitude
- Best practices for customer service over the phone:
  - Smile to elevate mood
  - Ask good questions
  - Show empathy
- Huge opportunity for companies:
  - Promote additional purchases
  - Build loyalty—73 percent of consumers say friendly service reps can make them fall in love with a brand (RightNow)

Now you've got the framework from which to write sentences and paragraphs that are arranged in a logical sequence.

Use a More Structured Process

Certain writers feel more comfortable with a clearly defined step-by-step process that they follow from topic development to finished document. And some instructors (not me) believe that writers should follow the same process for virtually everything they write. However you feel about that, a structured process can be an excellent tool when completing certain documents, especially the longer ones. If you want a process to follow, see the steps outlined in Tool 1-1. Modify the steps based on your own style.

Tool 1-1
A Structured Process for Preparing Your Text

1. Determine the purpose. (What is the situation, problem, or issue to be addressed, and why are y ou writing the document?)
2. Analyze the audience.
3. Identify the key points to convey.
4. Identify the action you want readers to take.
5. Develop an outline.
6. Write the first draft.
7. Revise the first draft for message, organization, and mechanics.
8. Make the document visually appealing.
9. Proofread.

Your Turn

You can use many strategies to get started, including answering your own questions, using a simple outline, and freewriting. To practice different strategies, try these exercises:

1. Think of the next email you need to write. From your answers to the following questions, develop a simple outline:

- Why are you writing this message?
- Who is your audience?
- What do your readers want to know?
- What actions do you want your readers to take?

2. Read over a report or lengthy email you wrote within the past six months. Imagine that you had just 30 seconds to explain the key message to a colleague waiting on the phone. Come up with the words you'd use and say them aloud. See if you got to the point faster in your imaginary conversation than you did in your text.

3. Review the freewriting below and develop a practical outline from it. Remember that certain points should be omitted and that some ideas may be repeated at different points of the text.

> Finally, yea, we're addressing a problem, three years what a pain in getting stuff in the hands of customers in the southwest states. So many of them have a fit when the products take as long as two weeks to arrive, can't have that no way. Everyone has their own idea about which city to open the new distribution center. Carlos Molina says Phoenix is the Mecca of the southwest, I don't know where he gets that from, aside from thinking about going to some Phoenix Suns basketball games. I'm not saying Phoenix doesn't have pluses, like an able workforce, so we could easily fill the jobs, I don't know maybe 20 to 30. Whatever city it is, we've got to move on it, management wants it fully operational by July 1 of next year, nine months from now. So decision time is upon us, by about start of Oct. Construction's gotta start no later than Feb. 1. At least weather is less of an issue in Phoenix, and with the other places in the southwest too. I say we hold a meeting with all the marketing and operations managers by this Friday, that's Oct. 5, discuss it, have everyone do their research and come back in three weeks so we can vote and get that decision done so we can move forward.
>
> Amber Nassar will be at the meeting. She's been touting Santa Fe as this enchanted city, she's traveled there quite a bit. Actually, New Mexico is known as the land of enchant-

ment, but who cares if they charge so much for rent, a helluva lot more than Phoenix for some unknown reason? Management wants good reasons for our decision, so we gotta go way beyond "enchantment." The best thing about Santa Fe is that they got the absolute perfect spot for the distribution center, I mean right off the highway and near a shopping center and if we ever have to visit, some outstanding pubs, but maybe I should leave this out of the next draft, I don't want anyone thinking my priorities aren't in the right place. Then you got good old Tucson, which has always had that weird quality to me. The guy in Chicago, I don't know him very well, Pete Marcus, thinks Tucson is hands-down the best place. Pros, the lowest rent and lowest construction costs. The cons, the location identified is hard to get to, 15 miles off the highway, on a treacherous two-lane curvy hilly road.

The Next Step

Once you've gotten your ideas on the screen or on paper, you need to write in a way that's easily understood, using as few words as possible. That's what we'll cover in Step 2 (Be Concise, Explicit, and Clear).

Step 2

Be Concise, Explicit, and Clear

Overview

- Use fewer words and sentences to convey your messages.
- Avoid misunderstandings with precise details and a logical order of text.
- Provide immediate context to enrich understanding.
- Stay away from stuffy language and buzzwords.

The more words you use, the smarter you'll sound! Although you probably recognize that's not true, you may instinctively—and often subconsciously—tack on useless words. These habits may have begun years or even decades ago in grade school and continued through high school and college, all to pad word counts and impress the teacher. But today, as working professionals, your readers (supervisors, co-workers, clients, and others) want just the opposite: brevity. This is especially true for busy CEOs and other C-suite executives, who need you to get to the point immediately.

Thomas Jefferson, our third president and an excellent writer who penned much of the Declaration of Independence, understood the importance of being concise. He said, "The most valuable of all talents is that of never using two words when one will do."

Wordy documents waste time—the writer's and the reader's. And lost time means lost productivity. To experience this firsthand, try this experiment: Time how long it takes you to read—and comprehend—paragraphs 1 and 2, one at a time.

Paragraph 1: In reviewing our latest renovation, we have determined that there were specific problems with the facilities in Houston. We believe that several mistakes were made that caused what amounted to a significant delay by our standards. This came about after a review of our records, which indicated that this renovation was supposed to be completed in a timely manner but was in fact three months behind the originally scheduled date. It was our determination that the delay was caused by several key factors. These included design that by all standards was considered inadequate and the submissions that were found to be late (completed by the engineer). In addition, the construction manager, according to our records, apparently didn't take any timely action to address serious deficiencies, which was also a major contributor to the problem.

Paragraph 2: The renovation of the facilities in Houston was delayed three months due to inadequate design, late submissions by the engineer, and the failure of the construction manager to address serious deficiencies.

It probably took you four or five times longer to read and understand paragraph 1 compared with paragraph 2. Multiply that difference by all the emails sent in a typical day, week, or month, and you've got lots of lost productivity.

Plus, imagine trying to read paragraph 1 in an email or a text message on your smartphone. At 134 words, it would show up as one long chunk of text, likely bleeding off the bottom of the screen. If you're like most mobile users, you'd scroll down once, realize the sender is wasting your time, and move on to another task. And even if you powered through all of it, you'd have to scroll up and down to connect the sentences together—too time-consuming. But with paragraph 2, which conveys the essential information in just 31 words, you could quickly read and understand the message.

Drop Unnecessary Words

Make every word, sentence, and paragraph count. Trash whatever doesn't contribute meaning. Let's start by getting rid of the "fatty" words in the following sentences:

Fat: In an effort to lower costs, we should order materials only from local suppliers.
Lean: To lower costs, we should only order materials from local suppliers.

Fat: Senior managers should work in conjunction with division heads to improve operations.
Lean: Senior managers should work with division heads to improve operations.

Fat: All employees must submit time sheets on a daily basis.
Lean: All employees must submit time sheets daily.

Fat: Hotel suites for the spring conference are completely filled.
Lean: Hotel suites for the spring conference are filled.

POINTER

Make every word count by deleting those that don't add meaning.

Dumping fatty words is easy, right? Just use your common sense to find and delete the unnecessary text. Now let's try dumping longer phrases and groups of words that don't contribute meaning.

Fat: It has come to my attention that the marketing department needs to hire two associates before we launch the next initiative.
Lean: The marketing department needs to hire two associates before we launch the next initiative.

Fat: I thought you might like to know that more than 25 percent of the support staff is expected to take vacations in July, based on the report from HR.
Lean: Based on the report from HR, more than 25 percent of the support staff is expected to take vacations in July.

Fat: Let me start by thanking all the operations managers, who helped our division exceed expectations.

Lean: Thanks to all the operations managers, who helped our division exceed expectations.

There are many unnecessary words and phrases that you may be tempted to use. Tool 2-1 lists some of them and offers lean alternatives. These will be particularly useful for any active social media account, whether personal or professional. Consider Twitter, which puts a character limit on tweets. By cutting the fat from your tweets, you're better able to pack your message with relevant information—or another hashtag. LinkedIn also limits the number of characters for updates, profiles, company pages, private messages, and other sections. And while Facebook doesn't limit characters, it hides content after a certain point, forcing users to click to see the rest. So with many forms of social media, if you're not concise, your readers may end up missing what you're trying to say.

Merge Sentences

Thomas Jefferson's advice about words also applies to sentences: One is better than two in most cases. While that doesn't justify run-on sentences, don't believe the myth that multiple short sentences are always better. For each of the following examples, the wordy version begins with a trivial fact (in italics) that doesn't merit a sentence. In the preferred versions, the trivial fact is woven into the meaningful information in a single concise sentence that flows more naturally. Read more about flow in Step 4 (Organize to Promote Understanding).

> **Multiple sentences and needless words:** *The September social media report was emailed to me yesterday.* I feel it's too vague. The report also exaggerates the number of impressions.
>
> **One concise sentence:** The September social media report is too vague and exaggerates the number of impressions.
>
> **Multiple sentences and needless words:** *At the sales meeting I attended, several issues were talked about.* These include the two most important areas: customer service and the lack of administrative support.

One concise sentence: The two most important issues discussed at the sales meeting were customer service and the lack of administrative support.

Multiple sentences and needless words: *The chief marketing officer reviewed our promotional strategy.* She believes it should be targeted to existing customers and to those who inquired about our products.

One concise sentence: The chief marketing officer believes our promotional strategy should be targeted to existing customers and to those who inquired about our products.

TOOL 2-1
REPETITIOUS VS. CONCISE TERMS

Repetitious	Concise
advance warning	warning
completely filled	filled
during the course of	during
for the month of May	for May
for the purpose of	for
honest opinion	opinion
important essentials	essentials
in an effort to	to
in conjunction with	with
in two weeks' time	in two weeks
located on, located in	on, in
merge together	merge
my personal belief	my belief
on a daily basis	daily
separate into groups	separate
the fact of the matter is	in fact
3 p.m. in the afternoon	3 p.m.
whether or not	whether

As you get in the habit of deleting unnecessary text, your number of sentences will naturally diminish, often dramatically, as in these two examples:

> **Five sentences:** The Q3 report is a bit incomplete. It needs more information on budgets. We need to know the amounts of money spent in the third quarters of the previous two years and how all those amounts compare with one another. So please make the necessary changes to this report. I do think it was well written, albeit without these key data.

To streamline, first identify the essential facts:

- Q3 report well written
- revisions needed
- omitted budget information from last two years
- need comparison with past two third quarters.

Then put them into a single sentence that eliminates the need for many of the superfluous words and phrases:

> **One sentence:** Please revise the Q3 report, which was well written but omitted comparable budget information from the past two third quarters.

In cutting five sentences to one, without excluding key information, you're conveying your point faster—exactly what the reader wants. In this next example, the impact is even more striking:

> **Seven sentences:** I know customer service training is critical. The problem is that I'm not sure about the training you suggested that will occur on October 10. For my team, we need to address technical skills, our biggest problem. In the past, they have sometimes, but not always, been included. My decision to enroll my team in this training is contingent upon the inclusion of this technical skills component. I'd appreciate if you could let me know either way. Then I'll make my decision, which also will be based on whether Anna's team will be able to cover our duties adequately on the phone on the training day.

To get to your point faster, identify the essential information, in this case the two conditions under which you'll enroll your team in the training:

- if it covers technical skills
- if Anna's team can cover phone duties.

Then, as with the previous example, write one sentence that eliminates the need for much of the wordy text in the first version:

> **One sentence:** I'll enroll my team in the October 10 training if technical skills will be covered and if Anna's team can cover our phone duties that day.

The difference: seven sentences with 106 words versus one sentence with 26 words—and far more readable text. We'll talk more about cutting in Step 8 (Edit and Proofread Effectively).

Be Specific the First Time

Readers prefer specifics over generalities, so don't waste their time providing both. Compare these two versions:

> **General, then specific:** With a comprehensive social media marketing plan, we can significantly increase the number of qualified new business leads in Q4 compared with the same period last year. Based on the latest projections, such a plan should result in a 20 percent jump in these leads during this quarter.
>
> **Specific only:** Based on the latest projections, a comprehensive social media marketing plan can increase qualified new business leads by 20 percent in Q4 compared with the same period last year.

By overloading sentences with generalities, you force readers to sift through junk before conveying the key information—in this case, the anticipated 20 percent increase in leads—which might cause them to perceive your message as less important.

Clarify So Nobody Misunderstands

Despite your best intentions, sometimes readers misinterpret a message that may have seemed obvious to you. So never make the reader guess at your meaning. Consider this example:

> **Vague:** Maria Ramirez is still waiting for your budget projections. Her deadline for submitting them to the CFO is around

the end of April, and they require two weeks to review what you've recommended. So please turn them in on time.

From that paragraph, the reader can't tell when Maria needs the budget projections. Here's one way to make it more explicit:

Clear: Please submit your budget projections to Maria Ramirez by April 14. She needs two weeks to review your suggestions and must turn the projections in to the CFO by April 30.

Here's another example:

Vague: Shipping costs for the third quarter were 20 percent higher.

POINTER

Never make readers guess what you're saying—they'll often guess wrong.

Were the shipping costs 20 percent higher than the previous quarter (second), 20 percent higher than the third quarter last year, or 20 percent higher than last year's quarterly average? If you're using a comparative term (in this case, higher), you have to say what you're comparing it with. Here's one way to clarify:

Clear: Shipping costs for the third quarter were 20 percent higher than for the third quarter last year.

Keep Text in Order

Don't let out-of-order text confuse readers. See how reordering words can clarify the meaning of the following sentence:

Confusing: Andy Ross told me June 1 that interest rates on the loan are 0.5 percent higher than anticipated, effective immediately, so please revise your figures.

Does *effective immediately* refer to June 1 or to the date this message is sent? The reader can't tell from this sentence and won't know on what date to base the revised figures. Rearranging the words in one of these ways will clear up the confusion:

Clear: Andy Ross told me that effective June 1, interest rates on the loan are 0.5 percent higher than anticipated, so please revise your figures.

Clear: On June 1, Andy Ross told me that effective today (June 10), interest rates on the loan would be 0.5 percent higher than anticipated. Please revise your figures to reflect this increase.

Here's another example:

Confusing: I need to speak with Oleg before his meeting today with the sales force at 2:30.

Do you need to speak with Oleg at 2:30? Or is Oleg's meeting at 2:30? Here are a couple of ways to clarify it:

Clear: I need to speak with Oleg today before his 2:30 meeting with the sales force.

Clear: I need to speak with Oleg today at 2:30, before his meeting with the sales force.

Let's look at one more example:

Confusing: The account manager finalized the deal with the software company using an innovative approach to mobile marketing.

Who had the innovative approach—the account manager or the software company? Here's a way to make that clear:

Clear: Using an innovative approach to mobile marketing, the account manager finalized the deal with the software company.

Put Your Message in Context

Never assume others know the topic or context of your message. At the moment they read it, they may be multitasking so they may forget the issue you're addressing. When writing to many readers, don't worry about offending those familiar with the subject matter. They'll appreciate the reminder, and your words will establish a context for messages that will be filed and referred to later. Compare these two sets of messages, each with and without context.

Message 1:

> **Unclear, no context:** I'm concerned that the project is taking too long, especially given the CEO's issues with the upcoming meeting.

Which project? How long is too long? What are the CEO's issues? What upcoming meeting, and when is it? Here's a way to write that so all the questions are answered:

> **Clear with context:** I'm concerned that the renovation of the videoconferencing center should've been completed September 16–two weeks ago–especially given the CEO's desire to finish it before the sales meeting on October 7, one week from today.

Message 2:

> **Unclear, no context:** You made the same mistakes again, and we need to get this estimate done right away so we can submit for approval before it's too late. Please revise and get it to me on time.

Which mistakes were made again? When did the individual previously make these mistakes? When is right away or on time?

> **Clear with context:** Your second-quarter estimate omitted travel expenses for the support staff, the same mistake you made on the first-quarter estimate. Please revise and submit to me by November 12.

Be Simple, Not Stuffy

One of the most prevailing writing myths is that simple and straightforward text will come across as unprofessional, particularly to supervisors and company leaders. As a result, many individuals use pompous language that lessens the impact of their intended messages. Busy readers—especially higher-level executives—want you to explain your point quickly and in plain English.

Considering the rising number of people who read emails and other documents on mobile devices, straightforward text is more essential than ever. Mobile readers have little patience for pretentious words or phrases that irritate them or can't be easily understood in the context of the message. Many will just stop reading and move on to another task on their mobile device.

Compare these sets of sentences for readability:

> **Stuffy and wordy:** Our team developed a new capability, incorporating a software program that facilitates the tracking of lead conversion at a 50 percent faster rate than they were during the course of last year.
>
> **Plain English:** Our team developed new software that allows us to track lead conversions 50 percent faster than we could last year.

> **Stuffy and wordy:** Our determination of whether or not to retain the services of the management consultant is contingent upon the completion of the evaluation process by the senior managers.
>
> **Plain English:** We'll decide whether to retain the management consultant after the senior managers complete their evaluation.

> **Stuffy and wordy:** You will be advised of my decision regarding whether our team will be able to meet the deadline that you requested on this project as soon as I review the situation with my supervisor.
>
> **Plain English:** After I check with my supervisor, I'll let you know if our team can meet the project deadline.

Tool 2-2 suggests simple, direct replacements for some stuffy words and phrases.

Tool 2-2
Stuffy vs. Straightforward Words and Phrases

Stuffy	Straightforward
abbreviate	shorten
accordingly	so
acquaint yourself with	learn
ascertain	determine, find out

Tool 2-2

Stuffy vs. Straightforward Words and Phrases (cont.)

Stuffy	Straightforward
as per your request	as requested
assumption	belief
at the present time	now
cognizant of	aware of
commence, inaugurate, originate	begin, start
consummate	close
conversant with	familiar with
due to the fact that	because
encounter (verb)	meet
endeavor (verb)	try
evident	clear
furnish	provide
inasmuch as	because
in lieu of	instead of
in regard to	about
in the event that	if
in the neighborhood of	about, roughly, approximately
of considerable magnitude	large
on the occasion of	when
peruse	review, study
precipitated	caused
predicated on	based on
prior to	before
pursuant to	according to
subsequent to	after

Don't Get Buzzed

Ready to *peel back the onion* for a *deep dive* into writing so you can *move the needle* on your capabilities?

These types of pompous buzzwords have permeated oral and written business communication in the past few decades. According to Robert Leonard, professor of linguistics at Hofstra University, workers use buzzwords as part of a basic human need to fit in (Kwoh 2012). While I've always discouraged the use of buzzwords, some participants in my writing workshops have shared that their colleagues and supervisors routinely include them in emails—so they follow suit.

Even if certain buzzwords and industry jargon are part of your organization's culture, use them with caution. These words often aren't the most efficient way to convey a message and may confuse readers. For example, the company's need to *pivot* during the next six months might have different meanings to different people.

The bigger danger with buzzwords is that the more you use them, the more likely you're sending this unintended message to the reader: *I'm trying hard to impress you!* As a result, you may come across as insecure and uninformed about the subject, which won't serve you well, especially with senior-level managers and C-suite executives.

Here are a couple buzzwords to avoid and more straightforward replacements:

> **Buzz:** To increase productivity, the shipping department should *interface with* purchasing managers.
> **Better:** To increase productivity, the shipping department should *work with* purchasing managers.

> **Buzz:** We need to *incentivize* the sales force to generate leads.
> **Better:** We need to *motivate* the sales force to generate leads.

Remember, don't let anyone tell you that straightforward language is too simplistic for the corporate world. In business communication, simplicity is your tool to achieve better results. See Tool 2-3 for a list of buzzwords and straightforward alternatives.

TOOL 2-3
BUZZWORDS VS. SIMPLE WORDS

Buzz	Simple
actualize	produce, make happen, achieve
deep dive	in-depth study
interface with	meet with, work with
bandwidth	capacity, resources
discuss offline	discuss later
amplify	improve
move the needle	make significant progress
drill down	examine thoroughly
above-board	honest and open
balls in the air	ongoing projects
face time	in-person meeting
heavy lifting	hard work
make waves	cause a conflict
north of	more than
red flag	warning sign
upshot	advantage, benefit
vanilla	plain, simple

Your Turn

Make cutting the fat from your text and using straightforward language a habit. Start practicing with the following exercises:

1. Delete the unnecessary words from each of these sentences.

> Her promotion will depend on whether or not she can meet her objectives.

Travel vouchers will be limited for the entire month of October.

Please create a list of our division's essential goals for next quarter.

2. Rewrite this sentence with language that's more straightforward.

We developed a new capability, incorporating a software program that facilitates the tracking of shipments at a 50 percent faster rate than they were during the course of last year.

3. Edit this paragraph to make it more concise.

Among the most important qualities of our leadership development program is its capability to enable those whose positions fall into the categories of first-line managers or midlevel managers to produce substantial enhancements to the overall productivity of their teams. In our opinion, this program will be able to show an increase, on the average, of 30 percent in team productivity. This result should occur within a 12-month time period.

The Next Step

Clear and concise text isn't always enough to keep busy professionals engaged. To carry readers along—in emails, text messages, and longer documents—you need a pleasing writing style and paragraphs that flow smoothly. That's what we'll address in Step 3 (Write With Style and Rhythm).

Step 3

Write With Style and Rhythm

Overview

- Strengthen your style with true subjects and powerful verbs.
- Keep your rhythm with text that's balanced, ordered, and separated.
- Enhance flow by varying sentence openers, structure, and length.
- Insert transitions to unify ideas.

"Get that rhythm!" It's great advice for singers, musicians, and dancers—and those who write everything from novels and poetry to activity reports and internal emails. The more your text flows with a natural rhythm, the more readers will pay attention and understand what you're saying. And the easier it'll be for you to create a cohesive, well-organized email or other document.

Rhythm starts with a strong writing style, which will enliven your text and subtly communicate to the reader that you mean business and can quickly convey your influential points. Style is defined as the conscious and unconscious decisions you make while planning and writing documents. These include sentence structure and length, paragraph type and length, organization, and use of graphic elements like boldface, underline, and italics.

Some of these choices are subjective and depend on factors such as your organization's culture, your readers' preferred style, and your personal preference. But other style decisions are more black and white and can reveal the quality of your writing. These choices can range from using precise language and sentences with the appropriate length (both addressed in Step 2) to avoiding excessive qualifiers like *very* to alternating between using *he* and *she* instead of exclusively *he*. (The other option is to use the singular *they*, which is now accepted by the AP and *Chicago Manual of Style,* among other style guides.)

Two of the most common style faux pas are using *there* instead of the true subject and choosing passive verbs or weak nouns instead of active verbs.

Don't Go *There*

Avoid using *there* when it's a false subject and replace it with the true subject. Compare these two sentences:

> **False Subject:** *There* are four more candidates who need to be interviewed before we hire a new procurement manager.

> **True Subject:** *Four more candidates* need to be interviewed before we hire a new procurement manager.

Unleash Verb Power

The verb is the most powerful part of speech in the English language. Strong active verbs, as opposed to weak passive verbs or hidden verbs (disguised as nouns), will energize your text. Let's look at some examples:

> **Weak:** Most of the senior leaders *are in agreement* that more dollars should be allocated to mobile marketing.
> **Strong:** Most of the senior leaders *agree* that more dollars should be allocated to mobile marketing.

The first sentence uses the weak verb *are* with the hidden verb *agreement*. In the rewritten sentence, the active verb *agree* replaces both of them.

> **Weak:** They *are* all *of the belief* that online learning modules can boost the performance of first-year reps.
> **Strong:** They all *believe* that online learning modules can boost the performance of first-year reps.

Here the passive verb *are* combines with the hidden verb *belief*. You can strengthen the first sentence by replacing *are of the belief* with the active verb *believe*.

> **Weak:** New hires should *have an understanding* of their benefits package after two months on the job.
> **Strong:** New hires should *understand* their benefits package after two months on the job.

Here the passive verb *have* joins the hidden verb *understanding*. The active verb is *understand*.

> **Weak:** Please take the account coordinators' suggestions under *consideration*.
> **Strong:** Please *consider* the account coordinators' suggestions.

Here the hidden verb *consideration* is combined with the passive verb *take*. The active verb is *consider*.

> **Weak:** The security manager needs to *perform an analysis* of potential cyber threats to our online retail operations.
> **Strong:** The security manager needs to *analyze* potential cyber threats to our online retail operations.

Here the verb phrase *perform an analysis* contains the hidden verb *analysis*. The active verb is *analyze*.

If those examples seem overly simple, that's because they are! Your challenge is to look closely at what you've written, find the weak and hidden verbs, and replace them with the corresponding active verbs. Then your message will come across more clearly and forcefully. Tool

3-1 will help you identify verbs hidden in nouns and replace them with active verbs.

TOOL 3-1
TURN HIDDEN VERBS INTO ACTIVE VERBS

Verbs Hidden in Nouns	Active Verbs
are in agreement	agree
conduct a study	study
give a presentation	present
give a promotion	promote
give a recommendation	recommend
give a response	respond
give permission	permit
have a preference for	prefer
have a tendency to	tend to
have the ability to	can
have an understanding of	understand
make a choice	choose
make a decision	decide
make an announcement	announce
make changes to	change
make modifications to	modify
make reductions to	reduce
perform an analysis	analyze
provide a summary of	summarize
take action	act
take into consideration	consider

Balance Your Text

You can immediately spot when something is out of balance: a crooked painting on the wall, a table missing one leg, or a man wearing one blue sock and one brown sock. And your readers can easily recognize out-of-balance text, although they may not be able to identify the cause. Still, they know they've been thrown off course and may stop reading or give less credibility to your message.

POINTER

Repeat key words and phrases to focus readers on your central messages.

One of the ways to achieve balance is through repetition, which is often misconstrued as always being a bad thing. In fact, some repetition can be effective. For example, using two clauses with similar structure or repeating words creates a pleasing rhythm, which makes a sentence more readable. Consider these examples:

STEP 3

> We prefer songs with a pleasing beat, and we prefer text with a pleasing rhythm.

> QY Partners won't improve its operations without hiring five new managers, and it won't invest in new staff without a leadership development program in place.

You also can use a balanced, consistent structure with two consecutive sentences, creating a natural bridge from one thought to the next:

> Last year's audit revealed that YK Industries was on solid financial grounds. But this year's audit revealed several gaps in its accounting methods.

The components of a sentence are considered balanced (and parallel) when the same word forms are used or when certain words or phrases are repeated, usually in a sequence. Here's an example:

> **Unbalanced:** All senior managers must train their direct reports to improve productivity, expense reduction, and address customers' needs.

In that example, the three areas that senior managers must train their direct reports on are not stated in a parallel manner. *Improve* and *address* are verbs. The second item in the list (*expense reduction*) is a noun phrase, so the list is not parallel. It's an easy fix:

> **Balanced:** All senior managers must train their direct reports to *improve* productivity, *reduce* expenses, and *address* customers' needs.

Changing the noun phrase *expense reduction* to *reduce expenses* makes all three items parallel.

Balance also applies to the consistent use of adjectives:

> **Unbalanced:** The new division head is thorough, fair, and displays honesty.
> **Balanced:** The new division head is thorough, fair, and honest.

> **Unbalanced:** Lois doesn't like long meetings or conference calls that are unproductive.
> **Balanced:** Lois doesn't like long meetings or unproductive conference calls.

> **Unbalanced:** We should recruit associates who are energetic, flexible, and have the motivation to succeed.
> **Balanced:** We should recruit associates who are energetic, flexible, and motivated to succeed.

To create balance, sometimes an extra word is needed to improve readability:

> **Unbalanced:** On April 10, the chief information officer explained the new software program, training schedule, and the most critical cybersecurity issues.

One of the three items, *training schedule*, is missing *the*. When *the* is inserted and repeated before each of the topics discussed, the meaning doesn't change, but the sentence flows better:

> **Balanced:** On April 10, the chief information officer explained *the* new software program, *the* training schedule, and *the* most critical cybersecurity issues.

Another way business writers wreck balance is with lists. They treat each bulleted or numbered item as its own entity, ignoring whether its format is consistent with the others in the group and how it flows from the lead-in sentence (more on that later). See how to balance bulleted text in Example 3-1.

Example 3-1

Use Parallel Structure for Bullet Points

In this bulleted list, the items aren't parallel:

> To improve communication, I suggest:
> - meetings conducted once a week
> - hold webinars each month
> - I'd recommend status reports to be produced every quarter.

The first item in the list begins with a noun (*meetings*), the second item begins with a verb (*hold*), and the third item is a complete sentence. And neither the second nor third item flow grammatically from the introductory phrase *I suggest*.

You can make this example parallel in just two steps. First, identify the type of word that must follow the introductory phrase. In this case, it can be a noun or a verb with an *-ing* ending. Second, write the bullet points so each begins with a noun (meetings, webinars, and status reports) or with an *-ing* verb (conducting, holding, and producing).

Here's the parallel version using nouns:

> To improve communication, I suggest:
> - weekly meetings
> - monthly webinars
> - quarterly status reports.

And here's the parallel version using *-ing* verbs:

> To improve communication, I suggest:
> - conducting weekly meetings
> - holding monthly webinars
> - producing quarterly status reports.

For more on creating effective bulleted and numbered lists, see Step 4.

Vary Sentence Openers, Structure, and Length

While repetition through parallel structure can create a natural flow between phrases and sentences, too much of it will quickly turn off readers. Here's an example of unwanted repetition in a paragraph, in which all the sentences begin the same way:

> During the first quarter, the absenteeism rate rose 12 percent, compared with the first quarter of last year. During this period, absenteeism was highest in the days immediately before holidays. At a time when keeping customers happy is critical, we need to reduce the number of unexcused absences. By developing a solution to this problem, our company will be able to improve client satisfaction.

How annoying! Beginning each sentence with the same type of phrase produces an unpleasantly repetitive rhythm. Let's look at some additional suggestions for changing up your sentences.

Don't Always Be an "I" Opener

Repetition is especially annoying to the reader when every sentence begins with the same word—like "I":

> I completed the external audit on June 20. I believe that XN Enterprises was not prepared to handle LZ Technology's requirements. I discovered that XN has no experience in the computer hardware industry and uses an archaic billing system. I think we need to conduct an online search for a supplier that has a track record in the computer hardware industry and an efficient billing system. I would be happy to answer any questions.

Now let's enhance the flow by varying the sentence openers:

> In the external audit completed June 20, I found that XN Enterprises was not prepared to handle LZ Technology's requirements. XN has no experience in the computer hardware industry and uses an archaic billing system. We should search online for a supplier that has a track record in the

computer hardware industry and that uses an efficient billing system. Please contact me if you have any questions.

The revised version covers all the same points that the rough draft included, but the reader isn't pounded with "I-I-I." The information flows from sentence to sentence and carries the reader along with it.

Break the Short Sentence-Only Habit

Writing a continuous string of short, choppy sentences also produces an irritating rhythm that drains your reader's energy. Read this out loud to feel its staccato and annoying beat:

> The annual meeting was held on June 10. Laura Ross is the president of our overseas division and spoke. She unveiled her marketing plan. She discussed several innovative social media strategies. The feedback on Laura's marketing strategies is due by July 1. We should meet to discuss various strategies. This should ideally be scheduled some time between June 20 and June 22.

It sounds like a 21-gun salute! This paragraph needs sentences of varied lengths and different arrangements of words (something other than subject-verb-object), and it needs transition phrases to blend the separate points into a cohesive whole that draws in the reader. An improved version has sentences that differ in structure and flow, offering the reader a comfortable rhythm:

POINTER

Listen to the sounds of your words to help determine how well your text flows.

> At the June 10 annual meeting, Laura Ross, president of our overseas division, unveiled her marketing plan. She outlined several innovative social media strategies. Because we need to submit feedback on her plan by July 1, let's meet to discuss between June 20 and 22.

In the second version, seven short, choppy sentences were combined to form three sentences. The first and third sentence use prepositional phrases: *at the June 10 annual meeting* and *because we need to submit feedback on her plan by July 1.* Between those sentences is a shorter sentence that varies the tempo.

Don't Go Long With Every Sentence

While a string of short sentences distracts readers, a paragraph with only long sentences of the same structure is equally difficult to read:

> Following our six-month analysis, we found that more than 65 percent of supervisors in the Northwest division lack core leadership skills such as communication, collaboration, and strategic thinking, which hampers their teams' ability to meet quarterly performance expectations, a troubling statistic that doesn't bode well for the future. Given this finding, we're interviewing three leadership consulting firms to determine which has the best approach to helping supervisors enhance critical competencies like listening, facilitating meetings, and writing sensitive emails. Once we select the most-qualified consulting firm, we'll conduct a conference call with division heads to identify the most pressing needs for these supervisors, a hotly debated topic, followed by a meeting with the consulting firm to clarify expectations, set objectives, and develop a preliminary timeline.

Not only is every sentence long, but each begins with a similar prepositional phrase: *after six months of analysis, given this finding,* and *once we select the most-qualified consulting firm.* That makes it tough to hold readers' interest. Let's see how variety of length and structure can enhance readability:

> Our six-month analysis revealed that more than 65 percent of supervisors in the Northwest division lack core leadership skills such as communication, collaboration, and strategic thinking, hampering their teams' ability to meet quarterly performance expectations. This is a troubling statistic that doesn't bode well for the future. So we're interviewing three leadership consulting firms to determine which has the best approach to helping supervisors enhance critical competencies like listening, facilitating meetings, and writing sensitive emails. Once we select the most-qualified consulting firm, we'll conduct a conference call with division heads to identify the most pressing needs for these supervisors,

a hotly debated topic. Then we'll set up a meeting with the consulting firm to clarify expectations, set objectives, and develop a preliminary timeline.

The opening of the condensed first sentence is no longer a prepositional phrase. The point on the troubling statistic was moved to a second sentence, now shorter and more impactful. The next sentence begins with the one-word transition, *so,* instead of the longer prepositional phrase, *given this finding.* The following sentence keeps the prepositional phrase, *once we select the most-qualified consulting firm,* which flows well because similar phrases were eliminated. In addition, this sentence was shortened so the key fact (that it's a hotly debated topic) isn't obscured by the next point (about the upcoming meeting with the consulting firm), which is now a sentence on its own.

Alternate Between Long and Short Sentences

So, which is better—short or long sentences? It depends! In some instances, short sentences are more effective, such as when you want to convey urgency:

> The client is livid! Nobody has replied to her email in four days. We won't survive with this type of service. Call her in the next 15 minutes.

But as we've seen, too many consecutive short sentences can feel choppy and disjointed. While longer sentences enable you to convey more information right away and let you combine data to reveal similarities or differences, you can lose readers with sentences that are too long. Choose sentence length based on your message, the tone you want to set, and your own style.

Let's look at a paragraph, taken from a performance review, with long and short sentences, a variety of structures, and transition words and phrases that move the reader smoothly from point to point:

> In three years as a customer service specialist, Nick has handled product inquiries efficiently, written comprehensive monthly reports, and trained hundreds of entry-level employees. He's a true asset to our team. Plus, everyone on

the team likes Nick and seeks his advice on many issues. Given his consistently high performance, I recommend promoting Nick to senior account manager.

Don't Interrupt Sentence Flow

If the main idea of your sentence is interrupted by a divergent thought, readers may get confused, as in this example:

> **Interrupted:** The accounting department found several discrepancies in our budget, in the May 1 meeting, which could short-circuit the entire project.

In this sentence, the prepositional phrase *in the May 1 meeting* pulls the reader's attention away from the writer's point. The writer wants to tell the reader when the discrepancies were discovered, but putting that information in the middle of the sentence may derail the reader. If that information is placed at the start of the sentence to give the message context, however, the reader's attention remains on the writer's key point—discrepancies that could disrupt the project:

> **Uninterrupted:** At the May 1 meeting, the accounting department found several discrepancies in our budget that could short-circuit the entire project.

Here's another example:

> **Interrupted:** The marketing director recommended several new tactics, which were all well received by the CEO and the executive team, including content redistribution, discussion engagement, and online contests.

Again, the phrase *which were all well received by the CEO and the executive team* interrupts the flow and diverts the reader's attention. In this case, moving this information to the end of the sentence creates a more natural rhythm.

> **Uninterrupted:** The marketing director recommended several new tactics, including content redistribution, discussion engagement, and online contests, which were all well received by the CEO and the executive team.

Don't Put Unrelated Ideas in the Same Sentence

This guideline needs no explanation. See how the unrelated ideas (set in italics) take the reader off track in the following examples:

> We need to recruit more experienced customer service specialists for the southeast division, *which just celebrated its second year at the new building.*

> The marketing team, *which has moved two floors up to a quieter location,* doesn't understand the subtleties of our new product.

> YBS Enterprises, *founded in 1949 in a Kansas City garage,* complained about our technical support five times this month.

In the context of your message, who cares about the anniversary of the building, on what floor the marketing department resides, or where and when YBS was founded? If you've got a reason to convey each of these facts, start a new sentence or paragraph and explain the relevance. Don't risk losing your readers' attention or confusing them.

Use Transitions to Unify Text

Within an email or document, each sentence and paragraph is not an island but part of a larger set of thoughts that need to be connected. Transition words and phrases—connectors—bridge one sentence to the next and one paragraph with the next, creating a logical flow of text that helps keep readers' attention. They include words and phrases that are typically used to connect thoughts (see Tool 3-2) and that provide natural connections when they're repeated throughout the document.

POINTER

Use transition words and phrases to unify the sentences, paragraphs, and sections of your document.

TOOL 3-2

WORDS AND PHRASES COMMONLY USED AS TRANSITIONS

Purpose	Word or Phrase
To contrast	although, but, conversely, except, however, on the other hand, otherwise, still, whereas
To indicate results	as a result, consequently, so, thus
To indicate time or sequence	after, before, during, finally, first, later, soon, subsequently, then, until
To introduce another point	also, besides, if, in addition, plus, with
To prove a point	because, for the same reason
To give an example	for example, for instance, in this case, such as

First, let's insert some typical transition terms to see how they improve a choppy paragraph that's trying to convey one idea with unconnected sentences:

Choppy: You should try writing like you speak to write better. You can do it when you start your next email. You should imagine that your boss is phoning from the airport and has only one minute to find out what you're about to write. This type of demand would force you to be concise and immediately state the most important points. This is how you should approach every document. It's true that most people who read your text don't have to board planes in 60 seconds. They're just impatient.

Unified and flowing: If you'd like to write as well as you speak, try this: Before starting your next email, imagine that your boss is phoning from the airport with only one minute to find out what you're about to write. Now, you're forced to be concise and immediately state the most important points—and that's how you should approach every email. Although most people who read your text don't have to board planes in 60 seconds, they're still impatient.

Repeat Key Points

By repeating certain words and phrases, you keep readers focused and remind them of your key messages. In the following paragraphs, taken from a service proposal, three key points recur throughout (set in italics and accompanied by a bracketed number to help you connect them from paragraph to paragraph). Although these phrases aren't identical in each paragraph, they convey the same points.

> The ABC Association plays a critical role in the insurance industry and offers *outstanding value [1]* to its members— but many people don't know this. The association needs to convey this and related *critical messages [2]* to its members, prospects, legislators, and other key audiences. These targeted groups must understand the *member benefits [3]* that are available.
>
> With its extensive experience working for the insurance industry, XYZ Marketing can craft the association's *key messages [2]* and help convey the *exceptional value [1]* that ABC Association offers. Among the *member benefits [3]* we would highlight are the association's legislative initiatives, educational programs, job training, and networking.
>
> By integrating tactics such as email blasts, social media marketing, and search engine optimization, we will deliver these *vital messages [2]* about the association's industry prominence and the many *benefits of membership [3]*. In the end, this will help build a powerful brand for an association that offers *superior value [1]* to its members.

Your Turn

To develop rhythm in your writing, notice when you read text with a pleasing flow from those you consider to be superior writers, including journalists, authors, bloggers, or even co-workers. Analyze what they've done to create that smooth stream of ideas and consider adopting some of that style in your own writing. And try these exercises:

1. Edit these sentences to create a balanced structure:

> Every quarter, the chief procurement officer meets with her staff to explain the purchasing protocol, supplier selection process, and the best cost-cutting strategies.

> The chief financial officer told the division heads to reduce expenses, to develop cost-savings measures, and that their unnecessary travel should be eliminated.

> The art director was asked to create mobile ads that were engaging, relevant, and projected emotional appeal.

2. Revise the order of ideas in this paragraph so the flow isn't interrupted:

> The social media manager recommended many new tactics for next year, which were all well received by the vice president of marketing and the CEO. These included brand advocacy, cross-channel campaigns, and native advertising.

3. Insert transition words into this paragraph to help unify the text.

> Wiring money is a relatively simple procedure. Many of Main Street Bank's customers had for several years been making errors that delayed the completion of their transfers. Mixing up the routing and account numbers was an example of the common mistakes they made. The bank emailed one-page wire transfer instructions to customers two years ago. It found that 30 percent fewer errors were made by customers since the guidelines were introduced.

The Next Step

Writing sentences with a pleasing rhythm makes it easier for readers to move through your text and understand your message. To further help readers grasp information quickly in emails and documents of varied length, you need to organize the content in a logical structure from start to finish. That's what we'll cover in Step 4 (Organize to Promote Understanding).

STEP 3

Step 4

Organize to Promote Understanding

Overview

- Start with the bottom line to hook readers.
- Separate ideas into manageable chunks.
- Create effective bulleted and numbered lists.
- Choose the best method to organize your document.
- Produce visually appealing text.

Even if your email or document is clear, concise, and explicit with a natural rhythm, you won't hold readers' attention and get them to embrace your ideas without a logical and coherent structure.

You may want to start by training your mind to select and differentiate bits of information when you hear or read them. Before you begin writing, jot down the key ideas you need to get across. If you've started with a freewriting exercise, go through your first draft, pick out your key points, and move them around to create order (see the outlines discussed in Step 1).

In this step, we'll discuss essential strategies for creating a cohesive document. When you get used to applying these techniques, you'll find that writing in an organized fashion will become a more instinctive process.

Start With the Bottom Line

If you're reading a novel, you wouldn't want the author to reveal the climax at the beginning or even the middle of the story. But in the business environment, nobody has the patience to plow through paragraph after paragraph to find the key message. Most readers want the bottom line immediately.

Journalists, having always recognized the urgency of enticing readers, routinely organize their stories to open with compelling leads that capture your attention. On the front page of the print or online versions of daily newspapers, you'll find this type of one-sentence summary of a story:

> ABC Industries rejected a $2 billion takeover offer from rival YZ Company, pointing to antitrust concerns, and reaffirmed its support for its deal with XA Partners.

No wasted words here. Notice the strong verbs like *rejected, pointing,* and *reaffirmed.* In a single sentence, the writer has summed up the key news, grabbed your attention, and enticed you to read the entire article.

Though you're probably not a journalist, you still want to capture the attention of supervisors, co-workers, clients, and others, most of whom are extremely busy. So use the same strategy: bottom-line your message, as with this sample first sentence:

> Given the latest data, your team needs to increase productivity at least 20 percent by the beginning of next year.

Now you've hooked the reader, who is compelled to continue reading your email and figure out how to become more efficient and increase productivity. The next sentence might direct readers to the specific strategies to achieve this objective:

> My recommendations:
> - Assess the six-month performance of each of your direct reports.
> - Determine whether some employees need to be given responsibilities better suited to them.
> - Consider hiring an experienced assistant manager.

You can use several approaches in the first paragraph to draw readers in. Typically, an introductory paragraph conveys one or more of these items:

- purpose
- situation or problem
- action required
- benefits for the reader
- anticipated bottom line.

For example, this introductory paragraph conveys the report's purpose and the action required:

> Our account reps have been underappreciated since I was hired three years ago. This report will explain how management overlooks their needs, why their training is inadequate, and the recommended steps to correct this injustice.

Here's an opener that presents both the problem and the action required:

> The annual conference is less than four months away, and we still don't have budgets, sales goals, sponsorship packages, or travel plans. Each of you must give me this information for your division by July 10. Please follow the guidelines outlined below.

This opener explains the problem of declining sales and clearly spells out how to reverse this trend:

> The 15 percent reduction in sales of building materials during the third quarter was due to the slowdown in new construction, colder-than-normal weather, and the lack of repeat orders from longtime customers. To get our numbers back up to second-quarter levels or higher, we need to expand our market geographically, better train the sales force, and increase email marketing by 25 percent.

In the opening of this email, the first few words tell the readers what they'll gain from taking the requested action:

> To help you and other line managers work more efficiently, we've retained a management consulting firm specializing

in time management. On October 11, we'll start offering online tutorials. Don't miss this opportunity to increase your productivity. Below are the schedule and registration instructions.

Separate Your Ideas

One of the most frequent organizing mistakes business writers make is scattering information randomly throughout the text instead of dividing it into single-point paragraphs and sections. The challenge is to not automatically present ideas the same way you processed them, either from another source or from your own mind—because they probably won't be in a logical order.

For example, when writing a review of a recent meeting or an industry analysis, you shouldn't just spew out fact after fact. Sort the information and separate it into chunks—typically with one idea per paragraph or one idea per section. This chunking process makes it much easier for you to put the material into proper context and increases the likelihood that the reader will stick with your text and understand it.

Let's look at an example where the writer has scattered her ideas all over the place:

POINTER

Each paragraph or section should address only one idea.

Ming,

Thanks for your input in this morning's extremely productive breakfast meeting. Following is a review of the key points we discussed.

I'm excited about your aggressive sales goals for the next year. Plus, I agree that customer service needs to be improved.

We'll be able to talk about these issues during the 30-minute biweekly conference calls we'll set up, which we'll start on February 6. From our end, our biggest challenge to improve customer service is changing the attitudes of our phone reps, who don't give your customers the time they need to resolve their issues. Starting January 15, all service reps will undergo a three-month online training that will address attitudes and the need to understand your mission to exceed customers' expectations.

All customer issues should also be discussed on that first call, especially the report on customer surveys that have labeled our reps surly, rude, and curt. The calls also will enable your team leaders to get acquainted with our customer service managers. Again, our company is doing everything possible to help you achieve these goals cost-effectively. You'll get a cost estimate by January 30, so we can move forward as soon as possible.

Please contact me if you have any questions.

Regards,
Paula

If we reorganize that confusing message by separating the ideas into distinct paragraphs, we produce a much more readable email:

Ming,

Thanks for your input in this morning's extremely productive breakfast meeting. Following is a review of the key points we discussed.

First, I'm excited about your aggressive sales goals for the next year, and we're committed to helping you reach your goals. Doing so will take additional staffing on our end. I'll see that you get a cost estimate by January 30 so we can move forward as soon as possible. Our company is doing everything we can to help you achieve your goals cost-effectively.

Second, we agree that customer service needs to be improved. This requires changing the attitudes of our phone reps, who don't give your customers the time they need to resolve their issues. In customer surveys, our reps have been labeled surly, rude, and curt. Starting January 15, all service reps will undergo a three-month online training that will address attitudes and the need to achieve your mission of exceeding customers' expectations.

Third, the biweekly conference calls will be critical in addressing all service issues and will enable your team leaders to get acquainted with our customer service managers. We'll schedule 30-minute calls every other Wednesday at 8:30 a.m., starting February 6.

Please contact me if you have any questions.

Regards,
Paula

In the revised version, each paragraph addresses a distinct issue, which makes the information easier for the reader to manage. Notice how each topic sentence sets the tone and establishes the context for the rest of the paragraph:

- First, I'm excited about your aggressive sales goals for the next year, and we're committed to helping you reach your goals.
- Second, we agree that customer service needs to be improved.
- Third, the biweekly conference calls will be critical in addressing all service issues and will enable your team leaders to get acquainted with our customer service managers.

By starting every section or new paragraph (or group of paragraphs on the same subject) with a topic sentence, you're telling readers where you're going.

Use Subheads to Highlight Each Idea

To further separate ideas and clue your readers to where you're going next, write subheads before each major section. Even in short email messages, subheads can enable readers to grasp your message faster. Plus, subheads eliminate one of the biggest obstacles to readability—the dreaded blob of text.

Take some time to read this paragraph:

I have several suggestions for marketing the new line of services over the next 12 months. First, we should place full-page, four-color magazine ads for the entire year in the five most important trade publications, which are all monthlies. Cost: $150,000. Another suggestion is to create a search engine optimization campaign tied to services that appeal to targeted industries. Cost: $50,000. Plus, we should send three email blasts targeted to all who previously purchased our services or expressed interest in similar services online over the last two years. Cost: $35,000. Let's not forget traditional direct mail. We should send product flyers to existing customers of all services every other month. Cost: $50,000. And I'd recommend that we schedule four educational breakfast seminars, in March, May, September, and November. We would secure outside speakers and hold the events at upscale venues in the southwest region. Cost: $75,000. Let me know what you think of these ideas so we can move forward.

To the reader, that paragraph is a big blob of dark spots that goes on too long without a break—it's a turnoff. But inserting subheads to separate the marketing tactics dramatically improves the appearance and readability:

I have several suggestions for marketing the new services over the next 12 months:

Magazine Ads
Place full-page, four-color magazine ads to run all 12 months in the five most important trade publications. Cost: $150,000.

POINTER

Use subheads that are explicitly related to the topic to draw your readers to your message.

Search Engine Optimization
Create a campaign tied to services that appeal to targeted industries. Cost: $50,000.

Email Blasts
Send three email blasts to everyone who previously purchased our services or expressed interest in similar services online over the past two years. Cost: $35,000.

Traditional Direct Mail
Send flyers on all services to existing customers every other month. Cost: $50,000.

Breakfast Seminars
Schedule four educational seminars on topics related to our key services, inviting outside speakers, at upscale venues in the southwest region. Cost: $75,000

Let me know what you think of these ideas so we can move forward.

With those subheads, the reader immediately sees the five suggestions and can choose which one to review first. For paragraphs or sections with more substantive information, use subheads that are explicit, summarizing the key points conveyed. These act like newspaper headlines that lure readers to your ideas.

For certain documents—such as proposals and reports—consider explicit subheads to increase the likelihood that others will read the sections of the text that follow. As an example, your division head would be more enthused about a paragraph with the subhead, "Mobile Marketing Can Boost Leads 35 Percent," than just "Mobile Marketing."

Tool 4-1 compares the ordinary and explicit subheads used in a proposal for new security software. Whereas the subheads on the left offer a broad overview of the text to follow, the ones on the right specify the key message expressed in that section, enticing readers to learn more. For example, instead of the general subhead "Integration," the explicit subhead describes the benefit: "Seamlessly Integrates With Document-Management Systems."

TOOL 4-1

ORDINARY VS. EXPLICIT SUBHEADS IN A PROPOSAL FOR A NEW SECURITY SYSTEM

Ordinary	Explicit
Security Breaches	Number of Security Breaches Doubled in Six Months
Intellectual Property	Safeguard Intellectual Property
Software	Software Offers Security at Operating and Application Levels

Valuable Data	Prevents Unauthorized Copying of Valuable Data
Integration	Seamlessly Integrates With Document-Management Systems
System Support	Supports all CAD and Business Programs
Next Steps	Approve March 15, Install April 1

Build Effective Numbered and Bulleted Lists

Most readers find it easier to understand enumerated information—for example, the three marketing objectives, the four action items, or the five keys to a successful career. This can be accomplished in paragraph form or broken out into lists (the preferred option today). Here's a sample of text in which the writer has enumerated his points in paragraph form:

> The sales manager outlined three keys to generating new leads. First, establish a robust social media presence. Second, call at least 30 prospects a day. And, third, ask each existing client to refer two prospects.

Here's the same text with the points broken out into numbered items:

> The sales manager outlined three keys to generating new leads:
>   1. Establish a robust social media presence.
>   2. Call at least 30 prospects a day.
>   3. Ask each existing client to refer two prospects.

Use numerals when the sentence that introduces a list cites the number of items in the list (as in the previous example), or when you want to present items in priority or order, as in these instructions:

Here are the next steps for relocating the warehouse from Denver to Colorado Springs:

1. Inventory all Denver merchandise.
2. Pack merchandise in boxes.
3. Get clearance that Colorado Springs is ready for shipment.
4. Ship all boxes to Colorado Springs.
5. Inspect merchandise for damage immediately on arrival in Colorado Springs.

When the number or order of items isn't an issue, use bullets:

In Q2, we'll need to hire new employees for these departments:
- finance
- information technology
- marketing
- purchasing.

Create Subcategories for Long Bulleted Lists

If you've ever read an extensive list of bulleted items, you know how difficult it is to take in all the information and how quickly you can lose interest. By dividing the list into categories with simple subheads, you make it much easier for readers to process. See the two following versions:

The marketing team has determined that these products will produce the highest sales margins:
- MP3 players
- slow cookers
- motion alarms
- LED security lights
- keyless entry systems
- blenders
- video game consoles
- indoor electric grills
- action cameras
- microwave ovens
- smartwatches.

Now consider this second version, with the 11 products divided into three subcategories:

The marketing team has determined that these products will produce the highest margins:

- Personal electronics
  - action cameras
  - MP3 players
  - smartwatches
  - video game consoles.
- Kitchen appliances
  - blenders
  - slow cookers
  - indoor electric grills
  - microwave ovens.
- Home security
  - keyless entry systems
  - LED security lights
  - motion alarms.

When you believe your bulleted list has too many items for one general category, create logical subcategories to help your readers grasp the message faster.

Frame Bulleted or Numbered Text

Before listing a series of items, frame them to provide clear context (as with the examples in the prior section). Otherwise, readers may be confused about the significance or the action step. Compare these two lead-ins to bulleted text, one vague and one clear:

> Our division fell short with managing finances and needs to do better:
> - fees associated with our three suppliers
> - ideas for lowering shipping expenses
> - anticipated raw materials costs for the next 12 months.

This leaves the reader with questions: Has anyone begun working on these tasks? Do you want me to complete them? Will I get any help?

Here's one way to clarify:

> To help our division better manage finances, please email me this information by December 15:
> - fees associated with our three suppliers

- ideas for lowering shipping expenses
- anticipated raw materials costs for the next 12 months.

One caveat for numbers and bullets: Use them sparingly. Nobody wants to read page after page of only lists. Intersperse them with paragraph text for maximum impact.

Organize With the Managerial Method

One of the most straightforward, yet powerful, ways to organize information is the managerial method, illustrated by this simple outline:

1. Overview or summary
2. Issues
   - Fact 1
   - Fact 2
   - Fact 3
   - Fact 4
3. Results and next steps

Let's apply this method in Example 4-1.

EXAMPLE 4.1
THE MANAGERIAL METHOD IN ACTION

Here's an example of the managerial method: an email explaining the problems with QV Associates, your company's marketing agency, during the third quarter.

1. Overview

Several problems were discovered with QV Associates in Q3, including an underpayment in commission rebate and creative and production costs that exceeded the budget. We need to further review QV's work so we can determine whether to renew its contract (expiring December 15) or find a new agency. Given our excellent relationship over the past five years, we'd prefer to resolve this issue and continue with QV.

2. Issues
- Billing and payment errors
- Commission rebate: $5,000 (should have been $15,000)
- Creative and production costs: $275,000 ($100,000 over the limit)

Additional concerns
- Previous overbilling errors
- No QV account rep dedicated to our firm
- Marketing manager doesn't understand terms and doesn't communicate effectively with QV

3. Next steps
We'll review billings and payments from the past 12 months and talk to key QV people to find out how the errors occurred. Then, assuming we're confident that the mistakes were due to misunderstandings or oversights, we'll suggest these changes:
- Instruct QV to dedicate one individual as client liaison.
- Ensure that our marketing manager understands commissions and rebates.
- Have QV schedule a monthly call to review figures.

We'll set up a conference call on November 20, 3 p.m. PT, with all parties involved.

Consider Other Methods of Organizing

In addition to the managerial method, other approaches may work for certain situations, based on the type of document you're writing, the content, and your personal preference. Common ways of organizing include:
- order of importance
- time
- space
- comparison
- problem and solution
- existing categories.

Organizing by Order of Importance

This approach is similar to the managerial method in that the most important information comes first, followed by the next-most important material, and so on in descending order of significance. It helps ensure that those readers who are too impatient to read the entire text will at least get to your key points. Journalists call this method the inverted pyramid and have been using it for more than a century to capture readers' attention. This method works well for proposals, project reports, reports of problems that need to be handled right away, and research findings.

Example 4-2 illustrates this organizing approach for a proposal to purchase new software. The example shows the critical points somewhat fleshed out, but not written as they will be in the final document. You could also jot down general descriptions of the points to be covered—these are shown in brackets after each specific point. That approach may be more useful if you're organizing your document before all the data are collected.

Determining which point is most important is subjective. For the proposal used in Example 4-2, you could argue that the old system's shortfalls are the most critical information and should be listed before the new software system. Only you know the specific details of your business environment and the personalities and roles of the readers, so use that information to prioritize the points in your document.

EXAMPLE 4-2
ORGANIZING BY ORDER OF IMPORTANCE

The critical points in a proposal to purchase new software might be organized in this descending order of importance:

- The new software system would save $250,000 in 12 months. *[primary benefit to be gained by the purchase]*
- The old system is too slow, has frequent shutdowns, and wastes operator time. *[key problems the new software will solve]*

- The new software received excellent reviews in key industry blogs. *[industry recommendations supporting the new software package]*
- The new system could be installed within two months. *[installation schedule]*
- The learning and development division could begin online training immediately after installation. *[training schedule]*

Organizing by Time

If your text deals with something that has just occurred or if it seeks suggestions or instructions for the future, let time dictate the organization. This method works well for incident reports, sales or trend reports, instructions or action plans, and company histories, among other documents.

Here's how organizing by time could work in a report on sales for a calendar year:

- First quarter: Sluggish sales in 10 of 12 states.
- Second quarter: Telemarketing helps increase sales 10 percent nationwide.
- Third quarter: Outreach to five new districts boosts sales another 8 percent.
- Fourth quarter: Sales drop 5 percent below third-quarter sales after industry downturn.

With a longer period to cover—say 75 years or more of a company's history—divide the years based on when events occurred:

- 1950–58: Mr. and Mrs. Carter form company and build it to 100 people.
- 1959–71: New owner expands to eight states.
- 1972–90: Four new divisions form, revenues triple.
- 1991–present: Merger with ZS Enterprises propels unprecedented growth.

For an action plan, the time-based categories would comprise the next steps in chronological order, with one or more paragraphs of detail after each numbered heading. This method of organizing is illustrated in Example 4-3.

STEP 4

EXAMPLE 4-3
ORGANIZING ACTION PLAN BY TIME

If actions are to be taken in a particular order, organizing by time is an effective method.

For a document outlining the steps a sales department will take in preparing for and capitalizing on the opportunities offered by an industry trade show, the action plan might be organized like this:

1. Set sales goals.
2. Develop traditional and social media marketing plans.
3. Approve marketing messages.
4. Get the budget approved.
5. Handle show logistics.
6. Attend the show.
7. Follow up on leads.

Organizing by Space

This method separates information based on different organization charts or geographic spaces, such as units, divisions, departments, regions, and countries. For example, a customer service report might be arranged by service territories:

- Mid-Atlantic: New software and training fuel 20 percent hike in customer satisfaction.
- Midwest: Departure of division head leads to 10 percent decline in customer satisfaction.
- Northwest: Customer satisfaction is down 12 percent after a team of inexperienced reps was hired.
- Southeast: Service holds steady for the third consecutive quarter.

Organizing by Comparison

This technique enables you to compare two or more topics. For example, a report comparing two divisions' performance in several categories might be organized like this:

Southeast versus Central:
- Sales

- Customer service
- Operations
- Employee engagement

As you can see by the example, that arrangement also creates a secondary organizing method (Southeast division followed by Central division), which is particularly useful if your topics are multilayered or complex.

Organizing by Problem and Solution

In its simplest form, this method presents the problem and then the solution. With multiple categories of problems and solutions, you should first determine the order of categories. Then you easily can describe the problem and the solution in each one. Here's an example that's arranged by company holdings:

Texas property:
- issue
- recommended solution.

Louisiana property:
- issue
- recommended solution.

Oklahoma property:
- issue
- recommended solution.

The problem–solution method can be modified to a strengths–challenges approach in a performance review, as with this example:

- Overview: summary of employee's performance
- Technical skills: strengths and challenges
- Phone skills: strengths and challenges
- Working with team: strengths and challenges
- Individual work habits: strengths and challenges
- Recommendations: promotion, probation, more training, more responsibilities.

You also can organize a performance review this way:

- Overview
- Strengths

- technical skills
- phone skills
- working with team
- individual work habits
- Challenges
  - technical skills
  - phone skills
  - working with team
  - individual work habits
- Recommendations

See more about writing performance reviews in Appendix B.

Organizing by Existing Categories

In some cases, the way you separate and organize information is dictated by natural groups. For example:

In the following report, the topics discussed at a marketing meeting form the categories:
- new slogan
- mobile advertising
- email blasts
- search engine optimization.

The different lines of coverage in an insurance company include:
- liability
- workers' compensation
- auto
- homeowners
- marine.

Which Organizing Method Is Best for Your Document?

If you're not sure which way to organize your text, begin sorting out the ideas—a process that can help you select the best method or combination of methods. Try these steps:

1. Identify the key concepts, using any of these means:
   - Write each idea longhand on a sticky note, index card, or notepad.

- Type your ideas in bulleted lists or other groupings.
- Create a diagram (using paper or a computer template) with various circles, each with one idea inside.
- Use an online brainstorming worksheet to enter your ideas.

2. Review the ideas and see if you want to add, subtract, or modify them.

3. Move the ideas around until you arrive at a logical order that will suit your readers.

POINTER

Base your organization method on the message, the content, the readers, and your own style.

In some emails or documents, the content may demand that you use a combination of organizing approaches. For example, you may be outlining an existing problem, describing the recommended solution, and proposing a timeline or action plan for implementing the solution. It's OK to use more than one organizing approach in the same document, but do it carefully.

Make Your Text Look Good

Creating a visually appealing email or document adds clarity and invites readership. Plus, an organized appearance helps you ensure that your ideas are organized. Here are some tips:

- Use short paragraphs. (This goes with the strategy of presenting one idea per paragraph.)
- Use bullets where appropriate—but remember that overuse can make your document visually displeasing.
- Set subheads apart with bold type, italics, underscores, all caps, or color.
- After a heading, insert a hard return instead of putting text on the same line.
- Skip lines between paragraphs or sections.
- Start a paragraph on a new page instead of splitting it between pages.

- Use at least 1.5 spaces between lines in a paragraph.

Use some or all of these tips to create a visually appealing document. (For suggestions on making text more appealing to mobile readers, see Step 9.) Example 4-4 shows how you can make an email message look good with headings, numerical categories, and further divisions with bullets. Notice that the first paragraph mentions the three sections in the order that they're addressed.

EXAMPLE 4-4
A VISUALLY APPEALING EMAIL

Brenda,

It was a pleasure meeting you last Tuesday. I look forward to working with you on the leadership training program. Here is a review of the key points we discussed, a suggested course outline, and the next steps.

Key points discussed:
- Primary objective: Get midlevel managers to foster greater collaboration with their teams
- Estimated budget: $75,000
- Timeframe: March 1 to June 1
- Training hours per month: 50

Suggested course outline:
- Defining leadership
- Evaluating leadership qualities
- Cases studies in leadership
- Role play
- Critique of role play
- Wrap-up

Next steps:
- Approve budget, timeframe, and outline.
- Determine enrollment.
- Reserve rooms and handle logistics.

Best,

Raj

Your Turn

Organizing your text requires many different techniques, depending on what you're writing, the audience, your purpose, and other factors. Try these exercises to hone your organizing skills.

1. From the information in this paragraph, create a bottom-line opening sentence that communicates the key information:

   > The recent performance evaluation at YB Partners conducted by our team of managers was spurred by YB's latest commitment to become more efficient in its operations. This initiative was mandated by Spiros Callas, hired six months ago as the new chief financial officer, who from the start has called on his people to improve their operational efficiency. Our team's evaluation found several areas that needed to be revamped, most importantly security, billing, and hiring. Our team concluded that correcting these specific inefficiencies would require YB to invest, over the course of the next 12 months, a total of $500,000.

2. Create an explicit subhead that would entice someone to read this paragraph:

   > Effectively managing email communication can go a long way toward enhancing your productivity. Start by reviewing your email practices and see where you can incorporate these steps, and even suggest some to co-workers. Strive to take control of email—so it doesn't take control of you.

3. Find the topic sentence that should've come first to introduce this paragraph:

   > Anyone in this company will tell you that the best charitable program we've been involved in was the United Way clothing drive the year before last, where 250 employees participated. Team managers want to ensure that next year's program doesn't take too much staff time. The CEO wants the human resource department to select a local charity to partner with for the next five years. HR has already received 27 suggestions from employees involved with worthwhile organizations. Members of the HR team should meet to

STEP 4

narrow the list down to five and then select one. The board has stressed that the charity selected must have a strong local base.

The Next Step

An organized email or document promotes clarity and understanding and helps keep readers engaged. When you want readers to embrace your ideas and take certain steps, you need compelling language and persuasive writing strategies. That's what we'll address in Step 5 (Persuade Readers to Take Your Desired Action).

Step 5

Persuade Readers to Take Your Desired Action

Overview

- Energize your text with compelling language and powerful openers.
- Address your reader's WIIFM. (What's in it for me?)
- Back your arguments with evidence.
- Don't just say it—show it!

If you want to convince a reader to purchase your product, hire you for a job or business project, or embrace your idea, the first step is to grab that person's attention. That's not always easy, given that the typical working professional is exposed to many thousands of messages a day—emails, text messages, social media posts, online news stories, mobile ads, and so on.

Communication theorists call this phenomenon *information overload,* which will continue to soar as we find new ways to produce and consume information. So how do you break through the clutter and get through to readers?

Start by recognizing how impatient most people are. Few are willing to slog through sentence after sentence to figure out what you're trying to say. Readers want text that's explicit and concise, with a clear action step (see Step 2). And they want you to get to the point immediately. Otherwise, they'll ignore your message and move on to the next one.

You can employ several strategies to stop readers and grab their attention, some of which are detailed in other steps in the book. These include bottom-line opening sentences, clear lead-ins to bulleted and numbered text, and explicit subheads (Step 4), as well as compelling subject lines (Step 9). Additional strategies will be described later in this step.

Another prerequisite for persuading the reader is an engaging writing style, which will enliven your text and subtly communicate to the reader that you mean business. Plus, it will enable you to quickly convey your influential points. For more on style, see Step 3.

Enliven Dull Text With Compelling Words

Let's face it: Most of what we write at work isn't thrilling—unless management reviews, mobile analytics, and corrective action reports excite you. The dry-as-toast verbiage of business writing pales in comparison to the wonderfully descriptive language of novels, memoirs, and poems. But we can't use flowery words to strengthen business text. Don't try recapping a meeting by writing that the chief technology officer wore an *exquisite orange paisley tie that complemented his finely tailored, single-breasted black suit* or that the *glistening sun lit the pudgy cheeks of the audit manager.* Save that for emails and texts to family and friends—or your next novel.

Still, you can enliven your text—not with extravagant or stuffy language—but with gripping language that engages the reader. Journalists use this technique every day to capture attention. See this one-sentence article summary from the *Wall Street Journal:*

> A surge in online shopping is reshaping New Jersey's indus-
> trial real-estate markets, fueling higher prices and sparking

development away from the usual hot spots along some of the state's main roadways.

Notice how the powerful words *surge, reshaping,* and *fueling* invigorate the sentence.

Here are a couple of business-world examples where dynamic words energize the information:

> The division head inspired the sales managers at today's meeting, challenging them to build relationships with prospects and address their long-term goals.

> In just three years as human resource director, Priya has fostered a positive working environment, which has helped boost productivity by 35 percent.

POINTER

Use active verbs to pump up the energy in your text.

STEP **5**

Sometimes, changing a single word can make a huge difference. Here are two examples of sentences instantly improved by compelling words (in these cases, metaphors):

> **OK:** The new five-year plan will *enable our firm to reach* new heights.
> **More compelling:** The new five-year plan will *propel* our firm to new heights.

> **OK:** XZ Partners' targeted online marketing *is helping it achieve* unprecedented revenue growth.
> **More compelling:** XZ Partners' innovative marketing is *fueling* unprecedented revenue growth.

Selecting words that enliven your text takes thought and practice. Use the thesaurus feature in Microsoft Word (Shift F7) or find one online, and pay attention to how journalists attract readers, especially in their opening sentences. See Tool 5-1 for more examples on reinvigorating your business text.

TOOL 5-1
BRING DULL LANGUAGE TO LIFE

Dull Language	Compelling Language
Large amounts	Huge sums
Means the workforce is changing	Signals a shift in the workforce
Do better than competitors	Outshine competitors
Could result in more sales	Could spur sales
Help them find everything in the employee manual	Help them navigate the employee manual
Is a result of her 15 years of experience	Stems from her 15 years of experience
Objectives that will result in higher performance	Objectives to drive higher performance
Make up for the higher costs	Offset higher costs
Get customers interested in our other products	Get customers clamoring for our other products
We want employees to like using the new software	We want employees to embrace the new software
Introduce a new training initiative	Launch a new training initiative

Grab Your Readers' Attention

Getting decision makers to pay attention to your email is a challenge, especially given the amount of information they're deluged with every day. Order your text so key points jump out at readers. (See more on organizing in Step 4).

The following email, which I sent to a partner in a public relations agency, led to a new business meeting. The first sentence addresses a critical trigger point for a typical PR executive—that substandard writing hurts productivity. Then the three bulleted statements focus on other trigger points: sparking media interest, breaking through clutter, and generating favorable publicity.

STEP 5

Dear Ms. Ronan:

Even some of the top PR pros today don't write as well as they should—and that can hurt productivity. If this is the case at ZZX Agency, I can help. I'm a 20-year PR veteran, corporate writing instructor, and professor. Having spoken recently on breakthrough writing for PR professionals at the PR Institute, I'm confident I can enhance the quality of your agency in the following ways:

- As a PR writing instructor, I can teach your staff to write more concisely, convey news value in just a few words, and write copy that sparks media interest.
- As an award-winning PR writer, I can ensure that releases, social media posts, pitches, and new business proposals break through the clutter.
- As a PR strategist, I can give your clients the edge over their competitors by crafting innovative story angles that generate favorable publicity in traditional and social media before their target audiences.

To learn more, please access my:
- website
- LinkedIn profile
- Twitter feed
- articles on PR writing

Satisfy Readers' WIIFM

Most working professionals fail miserably at persuading others to take a certain action or embrace an idea because they view the subject from their own perspective and neglect the reader's point of view. To win over one person or a group of people, you must answer the question, "What's in it for me (WIIFM)?" when *me* is the reader.

POINTER

Focus on the readers' trigger points to spur them to act.

For example, as the director of information technology, you want the staff to start using a new customized delivery management software application, and you send this email:

> We're introducing a new delivery management software program that will enable the leadership team to better track

results. It will be available November 1. An online training module is now available.

If I'm one of the employees reading this email, here's how I would probably react in my head: *Are you kidding me? I just figured out the current software. I've got no time to learn this new system!*

You haven't given employees one good reason to switch to the new software. Why should they spend their time helping the leadership team track results? What about their needs? What do they get out of it? Let's try again by immediately addressing the staff's WIIFM:

> To help you reduce your administrative time by 25 percent, we've developed customized delivery management software, which will be available November 1. An online training module is now available.

The first sentence opens with a direct reference to a WIIFM common to all employees—*reduce your administrative time by 25 percent*—giving them a compelling reason to learn the new software.

Tailor Your Message to the Target Audience

The better you can identify readers' WIIFMs, as well as their previous experiences, biases, and other factors, the more likely you'll win them over. For example, if you want your supervisor—who values productivity—to allow your team to work flexible schedules, then address this point in the first sentence of your email:

> We can increase our division's productivity by as much as 20 percent with flexible schedules.

Follow this with an explanation of how this flexibility would increase productivity, perhaps with additional facts and a spreadsheet.

While you can't know how every reader thinks, you can usually determine at least one WIIFM based on their role:

- **CEO:** If we open two new distribution centers, profits can climb by 10 percent. (WIIFM: profitability)

- **Operations manager:** By hiring five new directors, we can surpass our productivity goals for next year. (WIIFM: productivity)
- **HR director:** To boost our sagging morale, I suggest inviting the staff and their significant others to a social event every quarter. (WIIFM: morale)

Market a Product or Service by Appealing to Readers' Needs

Small employers can use this same principle to predict what's important to potential customers. Yet many businesspeople who know their prospect's WIIFM fail to address it in their messages. For example, a cybersecurity consulting firm that identifies a target company's primary WIIFM as protection against cyber breaches may send an email pitch with this opening paragraph:

> As a top cybersecurity consulting firm, YB Associates brings 10 years' experience providing top-quality protection against cyber breaches for all types of organizations. We would be happy to put together a program for you. Let's schedule a call.

In this opening, YB is doing little more than bragging about its services, giving the prospect little reason to continue reading. Here's a better approach:

> Your company's assets are too valuable to let cyber breaches get in the way. With 10 years' experience helping organizations like yours prevent cyber breaches, YB Associates can tailor a program to maximize protection for your assets. We would be happy to schedule a call and discuss your needs and potential solutions.

This version speaks from the prospect's perspective, opening with a strong statement about what the reader cares about: protecting the company's assets.

By speaking directly to readers' WIIFMs, you can overcome their objections, bridging the gap between what you want and what they need. Example 5-1 shows this strategy in action.

Example 5-1
Overcome Resistance by Satisfying Readers' WIIFM

Your ability to persuade readers may also depend on whether you can overcome their strong objections to certain positions, actions, or procedures. Consider this scenario:

> As a corporate trainer specializing in telephone customer service, you've been asked by the client's vice president of human resources to teach their reps to better engage customers, thereby increasing retention. In your initial meeting, she was adamant that no rep should miss more than two hours of phone duty each week for training. But to be effective and produce measurable results, your learning program will require the reps to attend four hours of classes per week for two consecutive weeks.

To persuade your client, you need to bridge the gap between your two positions. First, acknowledge her opposition to this additional time. Then explain that the additional training time will produce the desired outcome of higher customer retention—her most important WIIFM. See how the opening of an email might help win over the client:

> While I appreciate your need to minimize the reps' time away from the phones, my two-week, eight-hour learning program has proven to boost customer retention by an average of 25 percent. I'm confident that, in your case, we can increase customer retention by at least 35 percent within six months.

You would then include more information, including a detailed description of the training program.

Don't Say It—Show It!

Telling the reader that something is so usually isn't enough. After all, if you saw a restaurant's billboard ad along the highway that said, "Best Italian Food in Vermont," would you be convinced? Probably not. When writing persuasive messages, you need to *demon-*

strate your point rather than just saying it. Compare these two emails from management trying to convince employees that their feedback is valued:

> After researching several expense-tracking software programs, we're installing the EX-TK system, so please start using it by November 10. Your feedback is welcomed.

Simply stating, "Your feedback is welcomed," won't convince most employees that it's true. Many of them may view such a statement as the standard company line—mere management lip service.

Here's a more effective approach:

> After researching several expense-tracking software programs, we believe the EX-TK system will reduce your time entering expense data by 25 percent or more. Please start using it by November 10, and let us know of any difficulties you experience in implementation (email the HR department with "EX-TK" in the subject line). This way, we can make periodic tweaks if necessary and help ensure that future software implementations suit your needs.

This version addresses an important employee WIIFM—saving time entering data—and explains the company's effort in finding a software program that best accomplishes this goal. Plus, the language offers employees a clear path ("email the HR department") for providing feedback, which will be incorporated into future software purchasing decisions.

Back Your Position With Evidence

Whenever possible, lend support to your argument with whatever evidence is available. See the following examples:

> **Previous Success:** To improve our marketing return on investment (ROI) in Q2, we should launch social media campaigns in cities with rising populations. In Q2 last year, following a social media campaign in Austin—an emerging metropolis—ROI rose 25 percent.

STEP
5

Third-Party Facts: We suggest the purchase of InfraSup, a leading management software that monitors infrastructure, identifies the root cause of information technology problems, and reduces the number of redundancies.

According to an independent study by *Management Technology Magazine,* InfraSup has a 91 percent client satisfaction level, the highest in its category.

Valued Opinions: Our division should switch to the new cybersecurity protocol by February 1 so we can protect our networks, computers, and programs from mounting threats. Christina Kovatory, president of the Southwest division, said the new protocol has dramatically reduced the number of unauthorized access attempts in her offices since it was implemented six months ago.

Be Confident–Not Arrogant

Nothing turns off readers—and lessens the likelihood that they will accept your idea—more than coming across as arrogant and promising the moon. Plus, you may lose some credibility in the process. Compare these two versions of an email from a first-line manager to a supervisor:

> If we allow the staff to work from home one day a week, they will love us and their productivity will go through the roof!

Don't hold your breath for the supervisor's approval. Let's try again with less hype and more evidence:

> I suggest that we allow employees to work at home once a week. Based on interviews with them about preferences and studies citing productivity gains with work-at-home options, this policy should raise morale and significantly increase production.

That's more like it—a confident and professional tone offering evidence that the work-at-home arrangement will produce better outcomes. Even though the second example uses more words to make the point, it's written in a way that's more likely to appeal to the supervisor.

Your Turn

Getting readers to see things your way requires a combination of strategies. To get you started, try these exercises:

1. Find a recent article from a newspaper or online news site and identify at least three compelling words that help bring the text to life.

2. Revise this email to get employees to embrace the upcoming changes by focusing on their WIIFMs. *Remember, employees' WIIFMs (What's in it for me?) are to increase personal productivity and improve job satisfaction.*

> An organization sometimes needs to make changes critical to its long-term success. Effective December 1, this division will be restructuring. That means many of you will need to learn new roles quickly. The company sees this as an essential move to streamline operations. We're confident that you'll all make the required adjustments and become comfortable with the new processes.

3. Ask a friend to identify a TV series they've never watched. Then research the show and ask your friend a few questions about their TV-viewing habits and preferences. From this information, write the first paragraph of an email designed to convince your friend to watch an episode of the program.

The Next Step

Compelling and persuasive text is critical to get others to embrace your message and buy into your ideas. In many cases, you'll also need to convey the appropriate tone to ensure that readers tune in to what you have to say and don't get offended. That's coming up in Step 6 (Choose the Right Tone).

Step 6

Choose the Right Tone

Overview

- Select words and phrases that convey respect.
- Empathize when saying no or delivering bad news.
- Contain your frustration and offer constructive feedback.
- Always respond civilly, even to offensive emails.
- Tailor the tone to your reader.

STEP 6

On a recent visit to the Chester (New York) Public Library near my home, I was met by this sign on the door: "Food and drinks may be enjoyed outside on our benches." Wow, I thought, what a positive way to explain a rule while welcoming people into the library! The sign could've come across with the typical harsh warning, like, "Food and drinks are strictly prohibited in our library!" But that could've elicited a negative feeling among those entering.

The language you choose in your business communications establishes a tone that helps determine how positively or negatively your readers react and whether they'll take your desired actions. You've probably been on the receiving end of many nasty emails or texts and can recall how you felt about the sender. You may have thought, "Who do you think you are? If you want my help, forget about it!" (unless it's from your supervisor, in which case your opinion of them might drop considerably).

Let's turn the tables. You may have sent an email that at first appeared perfectly fine, only to be confronted by one reader with a response such as, "Are you upset with us? Did we do something wrong?" Then, bewildered, you review the language in your message and realize how it could've been perceived as offensive. And if one of the readers felt insulted, it's a good bet that many others did too. This is because it's typically more difficult to control your tone in writing than when speaking. The reader can't see your facial expressions or hear the fluctuations in your voice.

So think before you write—or at least before hitting send. Recognize that amid the stress of day-to-day work—when others often annoy us—you have a choice. Say your co-worker sends you an email asking for information, which you've already told him twice is unavailable. When replying, one option is to let him have it and make him feel foolish. While you may get five minutes of satisfaction, don't count on his support down the road. Your other choice is to explain, in a civil tone, why this information is unavailable and suggest some potential next steps. And if you believe this individual is not carrying his weight as an employee, then confront him in person or notify the human resources department. In most cases, it's better to resolve highly sensitive or critical issues through oral conversations rather than emails or text messages.

Select the Right Language

In many situations, you'll want to choose words or phrases that soften the impact of your message. When the point you must make might sting the reader, choose more amicable words to convey the same information. See Tool 6-1 for some examples.

On top of selecting the best words and phrases, you need to look at how the entire message comes across to ensure that your tone is appropriate. Let's look at a few common workplace scenarios and strategies for using supportive rather than offensive language.

TOOL 6-1
WORDS AND PHRASES THAT SOFTEN THE IMPACT

Stings	Softer Approach
This is unacceptable for submission.	This may be unsuitable for submission.
Your presentation was dull.	Your presentation could have been a bit more engaging.
Your proposal missed some vital points.	Your proposal should have included some key points.
You never returned my call or email.	I haven't been able to reach you.
I don't like your idea.	I have some concerns about your idea.
Your email confused me.	I wasn't sure how to interpret your email.
Your plan failed.	We had some difficulty implementing your plan.
You forgot about eight managers, who were left off the registration list.	Eight managers were left off the registration list.
You screwed up the report, just like last month.	The errors you made on this report are the same ones you made on last month's report.
I may be missing something in your report.	Please clarify a few points about your report.

Respectfully Ask for Clarification

If your co-worker emails you a draft of an industry report with many confusing sections, you may be frustrated by her poor effort and be tempted to reply with this opening sentence:

> Your industry report totally baffled me!

While you're giving an honest response, your co-worker, who feels put down, may interpret this sentence as: *You're an idiot! You can't write a decent industry report!* She may also view you as arrogant and unprofessional.

Here's a softer and more productive way to get your point across:

> Please clarify a few points about your industry report.
> *(Specifying where clarification is needed.)*

Contain Your Frustration

It can be extremely annoying when a co-worker requests information that you've already sent. But if you want to maintain an amicable relationship with this person, don't convey your annoyance—and belittle him—for what could've been an honest mistake. Consider this example:

> Why did you again request last quarter's social media analysis for LZY Industries? This was included in the email sent April 21. Here it is—again.

A better approach is to simply resend the analysis with a subtle mention (in parentheses) that the information was already emailed:

> Please see last quarter's social media analysis for LZY Industries (from April 21 email).

Then, if the co-worker continues to request information you've already provided, consider asking the person what you could do, such as using a particular subject line, to ensure that they open the email.

Offer Constructive and Thoughtful Comments

Say you received a proposal for a training program that's inadequate for achieving the stated objectives. Don't respond with this type of harsh, condescending email:

> I don't get your recommendation for one-hour training on capital budgeting analysis. There's no way 60 minutes is enough time. Remember, this program must cover complex issues like discounted cash flow and risk identification. For us to properly train these individuals, we must allot six hours—at a minimum. Otherwise, we're just wasting our time and won't achieve the desired results. If you want to do this right, contact me.

Notice the hidden insults that may offend the reader: *I don't get; there's no way; remember; for us to properly train; we're just wasting our time; and if you want to do this right.*

Instead, write your reply in a way that supports the individual's efforts to improve the proposal:

> You may want to rethink the proposed one-hour duration for the capital budgeting analysis training. Given the complexities of discounted cash flow and risk identification, I suggest that we extend the program to at least six hours so we can achieve the desired outcomes. Please contact me if you'd like to review the objectives and strategies.

POINTER

Don't be condescending when reacting to others' ideas.

Say "No" Tactfully

Sometimes you need to turn others down—for jobs, promotions, or other requests. But in the process, you don't need to disparage them with obvious or subtle put-downs, as with this email:

STEP 6

> Thanks for reaching out to us to request support service for your office in Memphis. Unfortunately, we cannot meet your request for the following reasons.
>
> First, you need to better understand our policies. If you don't put your expenses into proper categories, we simply cannot authorize them. At our company, we stress organization. Moreover, our experience has shown us that working with unorganized affiliates can seriously compromise our productivity.
>
> Second, which people would be working on which projects? Unless I missed something, I could not find this mentioned anywhere in your request. As we've indicated several times in our emails to your office, allocation of responsibilities in advance is crucial for us to authorize support services.
>
> Once again, we appreciate the request. Please keep in mind these guidelines should you decide to again ask for support services.

Consider all the condescending language and the potential hidden meaning:

- You need to better understand our policies *(because you're ignorant)*.
- At our company, we stress organization *(not like your totally disorganized office)*.
- Working with unorganized affiliates can seriously compromise our productivity *(you're not good enough to work with us)*.
- Unless I missed something, I could not find this mentioned anywhere in your request *(I can't believe you left this out)*.
- As we've indicated several times in our correspondence with your office *(you just don't pay attention)*.

Let's try again with a supportive, matter-of-fact approach without the offensive language:

> Thanks for reaching out to us for support service for your Memphis office. We cannot meet your request for two reasons. We require that the request be organized into proper categories and that allocation of responsibilities be given in advance.
>
> Please feel free to resubmit this request when these requirements have been met, and call us if you have any questions.

Empathize When Delivering Bad News

At one time or another, you've been a customer who has contacted a company to request a refund, rebate, discount, or another perk you believe is owed to you. When it doesn't turn out in your favor, you're annoyed, often with good reason.

POINTER

Empathize with the customer when turning down a request.

Now put yourself at the other end of the message, as a representative of the company who needs to send an email explaining to the customer why they aren't getting what they want. Good luck! First, recognize that you can't make the person's irritation and displeasure with your company disappear.

Then figure out how to temper your bad-news message to show that you understand the individual's concerns.

Following are examples of ineffective and effective ways to tell small business owner Marina Bowman that her HD projector is no longer under warranty and will cost $300 to repair. The projector malfunctioned just hours before an out-of-town new business presentation, forcing her to rent a projector at the last moment. Marina has sent an email, expressing her dissatisfaction that the product had failed just 15 months after she purchased it and has requested that the manufacturer cover the cost of the repair or send her a new projector.

> Dear Marina,
>
> With regret, I must tell you that your HD projector is no longer under warranty and we cannot repair the switch malfunction you reported. The projector is guaranteed for 12 months, and your problem occurred 15 months after the purchase date.
>
> We did offer an extended warranty for $39.99 that would have covered the machine for an additional 24 months, but you declined that offer.
>
> Our company apologizes for any inconvenience or unanticipated expense as a result of the machine's malfunction. We have many new HD projector models available on our website, and I'd be happy to have one of our sales reps contact you to discuss which is best for your needs and to review the extended warranty.
>
> Sincerely,
> Brian Oliver
> Customer Service Manager

This impersonal email blames Marina for not purchasing the extended warranty and attempts to get her to spend more money—not the best way to build customer loyalty. Let's try again with a more empathetic and genuine response.

> Dear Marina,
>
> What an inopportune time for your HD projector to break

down. I hope your presentation with the rented machine was successful—and that you turned the prospect into a client.

We do our best to build high-quality machines, but sometimes make mistakes in the process. Unfortunately, we can't bend the rules on warranties. I wish we could.

What I'd like to do is research other models in our inventory and offer you the best discounts available—those usually reserved for our large corporate customers who purchase 25 or more machines a year. I'll also offer the extended warranty for no additional charge, a $39.99 value.

Give me a week and I'll call you to let you know what's available and give you details on the discounts.

Please call me if you have questions.

Sincerely,
Brian Oliver
Customer Service Manager

This email empathizes with Marina's circumstances as a businessperson, expresses interest in her success, and commits Brian to an active role in solving the problem in a way that may satisfy all parties. Plus, it sets a much warmer tone. Notice that Brian does *not* get to the point right away. Instead, he begins by putting himself in the customer's shoes. While Marina still may not be thrilled, she sees that Brian and others at the company care about the people who use its products. For additional guidelines and an example of how to send bad-news correspondence to clients, see Appendix B.

Respond Civilly to Offensive Emails

When you receive a rude or condescending email, your first instinct may be to immediately respond with an even nastier email. You're thinking, "I can't let her get away with that. Let's see how *she* likes being insulted!"

Resist the urge to strike back harder—regardless of how much the incoming email infuriated you—because you may soon regret such an impulsive action. If you need to let off steam, type out your counter-punch reply—but be sure to hit the Draft key. Or better yet, compose the text in a Word file to avoid accidentally hitting send.

Then give yourself time—at least 30 minutes—before rereading your potentially offensive email so you can reconsider the consequences and transform it into a more civil and productive message. Take a look at this condescending incoming email and compare the two types of replies:

> You need to email me the January figures on sales volume and accounts opened and closed by tomorrow at 10 a.m. so I can begin my analysis. I assume that you're aware of the critical importance of this analysis!

> **Inflammatory reply:** Are you serious? How about a little more notice? There's no way I can get you these figures before Monday. I haven't even received all the data! Don't you believe in planning projects ahead of time?

> **Productive reply:** I appreciate your need to complete the analysis as soon as possible, but I haven't received all the January data. What I could do is email you the figures through January 24 by tomorrow so you can begin your analysis. Then you can make minor edits when I submit the rest of the figures on Monday. Please let me know if this would work for you.

Know Your Reader

While documents and emails to all your readers should come across professionally and respectfully, the more you know about each person or a group of people (for example, your direct reports or others on your team), the better you can tailor your language to produce the desired results.

Readers may perceive your email or text message in different ways based on whether they're open, indifferent, or hostile (or a combination of these) to you. The more you can predict into which category a single person or group of readers fall, the better you can customize your language. Here are some strategies:

For Readers Open to Your Message

For close colleagues or others with whom you feel comfortable, a warm and friendly tone works best. Here's an example:

> You and I know our mobile advertising plan needs a major overhaul. Let's work on getting the marketing director to see things our way.

For Readers Indifferent to Your Message

With individuals who don't know you that well or who have no stake in whether your ideas are well received, address hot-button topics or WIIFMs (see Step 5). Consider the following example, which can be aimed at a CEO, division head, or other decision maker:

> We should invest in this new software program because it will improve productivity by 15 percent and free the sales force to generate more leads.

For Readers Hostile to Your Message

To get through to a hostile reader (like a dissatisfied customer) find common ground. Acknowledge and empathize with their concerns and explain your solution. Here's an example:

> I agree that my team's service has declined due to a lack of technical knowledge. Starting tomorrow, all reps will attend a 20-hour online training course that will help them identify customers' technical needs and direct inquiries to the proper department faster.

You can also adjust your tone based on your relationship with the reader in an organization, which can be categorized in several ways. We'll address the two most common: supervisor and direct report.

Writing to Supervisors

Through effective written communication to your supervisor, you can validate your competencies—such as your knowledge, analytical skills, and leadership abilities—and demonstrate the value you bring to them and to the organization.

First select the appropriate style (formal or informal) based on your supervisor's preference, which you can usually determine by reviewing their messages to you. And if you're not sure, ask. Always use respectful language, and, where appropriate, speak to what your boss cares about (see Step 5 on satisfying the WIIFM). This could include exceeding sales goals, staying within the budget, or easing pressure from higher-ups. It also helps to know your boss's outside interests and whether they have a sense of humor.

Let's take a scenario in which you need to choose words carefully to establish the right tone: Your supervisor is unhappy with your team's drop in production, which you attribute to the layoffs of two employees in the previous quarter of last year. She has asked for an email explaining the decline and your plan to bring production back up to last year's level. Your email should:

- Empathize with her dissatisfaction with production.
- Allude to the reduction in staff without making it an excuse.
- Exude confidence in your ability to increase production.
- Outline one or more steps for achieving this goal.

Here's how the message to your supervisor might read:

> Karen,
>
> As you pointed out, production must improve to at least last year's level—and we probably can do even better. The months following the layoffs of Olga and Rick have been challenging, but the team has begun to develop new strategies for increasing production. These include an advanced lead-generation system.
>
> Please review the details below. I'm excited about moving forward with this new system, assuming you approve it.
>
> Thanks,
> Miguel

Let's review what parts of that email delivered the appropriate tone:

STEP 6

- I agree that production must improve to at least the level of last year—and we probably can do even better *(conveys that you understand why the boss is upset)*.
- The months following the layoffs of Olga and Rick have been challenging *(reminds her of the reduction in staff, without making it an excuse)*.
- The team has begun to develop new strategies for increasing production *(exudes confidence in your ability to motivate your people)*.
- An advanced lead-generation system *(outlines one step for achieving this goal)*.

Writing to Direct Reports

Your communication to those who report to you plays a critical role in building your relationship with them and enhancing performance. Every email and text message to these individuals is a chance to demonstrate support, motivate, and enhance morale. Yet many managers fail to take advantage of this opportunity—and sometimes send messages with a negative tone that damages relationships with direct reports and ultimately lowers productivity.

Often this negative tone comes across when assigning work. Many supervisors who complete my writing workshops or coaching have shared that they're "too blunt" with these types of messages. Compare the openings of these two emails from a supervisor to a direct report about completing a project:

> **Blunt and bossy:** The XB project is critical, so you need to complete several tasks no later than January 30! The XB project is even more important than the ZD project you completed in December.
>
> **Appreciative and inspiring:** Thanks again for your hard work on the ZD project in December. Now we have the more important XB project, so I could use your help completing these tasks by January 30.

Another all-too-common challenge for supervisors is addressing mistakes by one or more direct reports. How you describe the situation and convey your attitude can play an important role in their performance and job satisfaction. Compare these two emails:

> **Negative, critical tone:** I'm appalled by the number of payroll errors you've made on the XW Partners' account. This client is vital to our company, and we can't tolerate such a lack of attention to detail. Each of you must attend a meeting this Thursday at 8:30 a.m. to review procedures so we can eliminate these mistakes! This is a mandatory meeting!
>
> **Productive tone:** Several serious errors have been made on the payroll for XW Partners, a vital account to our company. Each of you needs to be more careful. Please mark your calendars for this Thursday at 8:30 a.m. for a meeting to review procedures and develop methods to help eliminate errors.

Most employees reading the first email will react with anger, frustration, or another negative emotion that probably will make them less productive (at least for the rest of that day) and less committed to supporting their boss. The second email is more empathetic and sends a better message.

Let's look more closely at strategies for criticizing—and praising—direct reports in emails.

Be Specific With Your Criticism

When you need to point out shortcomings in those who report to you, address specific mistakes instead of broad personality traits (which probably should be addressed in a face-to-face meeting). Then clearly define the steps they should take to correct the problem. Compare these two versions of an email criticizing an employee's lack of attention to customer service:

> **Vague criticism and recommendation:** Anna Novak of ZX Enterprises says that you haven't been paying enough attention to her requests. We'll lose this client if you continue to be so nonresponsive! Your service skills must begin to improve immediately.
>
> **Specific criticism and recommendation:** Anna Novak of ZX Enterprises is upset that you haven't

POINTER

Be specific when you point out direct reports' mistakes.

haven't returned two of her emails over the past five days. Some of her staff hasn't been able to access the application we installed last week. Remember that our policy is to always return client emails within 24 hours. ZX Enterprises is one of our most valued clients, and we can't afford to lose them. Email her by 10 a.m. to set up a call to discuss how to resolve this issue.

Temper Your Criticism When Necessary

In some cases, you'll want to soften your negative comments to those who report to you. One way is to label a mistake as an example of a department-wide problem. And, if appropriate, you can remind this individual that they are an asset to the company, despite the error. Here's an example:

> Justin,
>
> Your high-caliber work on the ZYZ Railways project over the past two months has helped us increase productivity, including freeing up my time for other important projects. But you need to be more careful with the monthly client activity reports. In September, the report erroneously stated that ZYZ was two months behind in its payment, which upset several of its senior managers.
>
> I recognize that these reports are often copied and pasted from prior reports and that mistakes happen. In fact, many others on our team have made similar errors over the past six months. We need to put a stop to it.
>
> Tomorrow I'm sending an email to the entire team explaining the new protocol where every client report must be carefully proofed by at least two other people.
>
> Thanks,
> Marc

Give Broad and Specific Praise When Merited

Although flattering others can elevate their self-esteem and boost their morale, it can backfire when perceived as insincere or patronizing. If you praise an employee every time they do something right with statements like *Thanks for being a true team player!* or *Great job!* your message quickly will come across as phony and lose its impact. Then, when they achieve a feat that truly deserves a compliment, your kudos will seem disingenuous.

When a direct report (or a co-worker) has completed a project that deserves a compliment, include both a broad stroke on that person's value to the company and praise for the specific efforts that have paid dividends. Here's an example:

> Lorraine,
>
> Your projected budget forecast was well written, superbly organized, and comprehensive. You anticipated several expense categories I might have overlooked. Thanks for always coming through for our team!

Your Turn

Expressing the right tone is difficult in the stress of day-to-day work, especially when others annoy you or when writing to those who are upset with your company. These exercises will help hone your skills in writing with an appropriate tone in different situations.

1. Rewrite this email so it's respectful, rather than condescending, to the reader:

   > I don't really understand your request for specifications from a project completed four years ago. There's absolutely no value in going back more than two years, given how fast our industry changes. If you, however, really need these old specs, I'll see what I can do. Let's be sure we don't waste time here.

2. You just received an email from a customer who's angry that his snowblower broke when he tried clearing an 18-inch snowfall from his driveway. As a result of the machine's failure, the customer was forced to spend $150 on a plowing service. He wants the company to pay for the $700 snowblower repair, although the warranty expired three months ago. The customer

also wants your company to reimburse him for the plowing expense. Write a reply explaining that the company can't pay for either expense, while conveying your empathy with his frustration.

3. Your new client has sent you an email requesting a project for a fee far less than your company can offer. Revise this harsh and condescending reply in a way that helps build a relationship with the client—without agreeing to this fee:

> I'm puzzled by your request. There's no way we can offer your division all these services for just $25,000. Remember that we've got to incur quite a few costs, including labor, research, and travel. We need to set up a call and figure out how to raise this fee to a more reasonable level.

The Next Step

In addition to carefully choosing a tone that expresses empathy and produces the results you want, you need to exhibit your professionalism in the way you compose your text. That requires, among other skills, a sound command of grammar. We'll address that topic in Step 7 (Put Your Best Grammar on the Page).

STEP 6

Step 7

Put Your Best Grammar on the Page

Overview

- Recognize the value of proper grammar.
- Review basic punctuation.
- Learn essential grammar rules.
- Avoid common word usage errors.

Who cares if you omit a period or whether your noun agrees with your verb? You're dealing with more important issues like budget projections, operational efficiency, and social media analytics. Just say what you need to say and don't worry about a minor detail like grammar!

If only it were that easy. While one misplaced comma won't ruin your career, emails and texts laden with poor punctuation, misused words, and inconsistent tenses will distract readers from your message. Worse, you may be perceived as ignorant, sloppy, or lazy—even if you don't possess any of these unfavorable traits.

A simple spelling or grammatical mistake can lead your clients or potential partners to think twice about working with you. Social media is littered with compilations of embarrassing grammar errors—to the hilarity of online scavengers, the dismay of English teachers, and the ire of social media managers. So, even with the speed of online communication, a grammar faux pas can leave a lasting impression.

Using correct grammar makes your text easier to read and understand. And while no one expects you to be a perfect grammarian, you should be able to apply the key rules and avoid common mistakes. Your grammar should be like referees in professional sports—the less you notice them, the better.

Even those confident in their grammar skills can use the occasional refresher. But if you struggle with grammar, study the rules and examples that follow. They won't address more advanced aspects of grammar (such as gerunds, participles, and nonstandard verb phrases), but they will explain how to determine what's right and wrong in your business communication.

In many cases, you don't need to memorize grammar rules; just use common sense. For rules not addressed in this step, consult a grammar website, such as www.grammarbook.com, or Google the issue.

Punctuate It Right

Let's start by reviewing punctuation marks you probably use hundreds of times a day in your business and personal communication.

Period

Insert a period at the end of a complete sentence:

> She led the time management training.

Don't repeat a period if the last item of the sentence is an abbreviation that ends in a period:

> Meet Claire at 10:30 a.m.

If the sentence ends with a question mark or exclamation point you don't need a period:

> Your team was outstanding!

Comma

Commas separate independent clauses (complete sentences) that are joined by a conjunction:

> I'll help you with the benefits analysis, but I don't have time to call the client.

They also separate an introductory phrase or clause:

> Given the complexity of the report, we should get additional help.

Use a comma to set off a phrase describing the subject:

> Chen Lee, hired three months ago, has become an asset to our team.

Commas are always placed inside quotation marks:

> "The last shipment was three days late," she told her boss.

Set apart items in a series using commas:

> The senior partner discussed new practice areas, marketing strategies, and operations.

The last comma before the conjunction *and*—the serial or Oxford comma—is either required or omitted depending on your preferred style guide. The *Chicago Manual of Style* is for it, while the *Associated Press Stylebook* excludes the comma unless it's essential to avoid confusion. See this example:

> The mechanical engineer met with three senior executives, two vice presidents and one division head.

Did the engineer meet with three executives—two who were vice presidents and one who was a division head? Or did the engineer meet with six people—three executives, two vice presidents, and a division head? If it was six people, then the serial or Oxford comma needs to follow *vice presidents* for clarification:

The mechanical engineer met with three senior executives, two vice presidents, and one division head.

If you don't believe commas matter, compare the two meanings in each of these pairs of sentences:

Let's eat Aunt Margaret. *(What?)*
Let's eat, Aunt Margaret. *(That's more like it!)*

Rachael Ray finds inspiration in cooking her family and her dog. *(Is she serious?)*
Rachael Ray finds inspiration in cooking, her family, and her dog. *(Much better!)*

While *Tails* magazine correctly inserted the commas in its article about celebrity chef Rachael Ray, a parody of this statement went viral on the Internet a few years ago.

Colon

Colons indicate a stop followed by an explanation:

He figured out how to impress his boss: Complete the web analytics report one week early.

Colons also indicate a stop followed by a list:

The HR executive explained the keys to success: hard work, flexibility, and collaboration with the team.

However, never use a colon directly following a verb:

Wrong: XCL Consulting's services include: performance improvement, sustainability, customer strategy, and advanced analytics.
Right: XCL Consulting's services include performance improvement, sustainability, customer strategy, and advanced analytics.

Semicolon

Use a semicolon to join two sentences with a similar construction:

Her audit report last month was 20 pages; this month's document was only 12 pages.

Semicolons are used to avoid confusion when items in a series contain commas:

> Our event planner visited potential conference sites in Charleston, West Virginia; Portland, Maine; Fort Collins, Colorado; and Spokane, Washington.

Hyphen

Hyphens join two or more words that serve as an adjective modifying a noun:

> The division head wants the second day of the annual meeting to be divided into three-hour sessions.

Without the hyphen between three and hour, your meaning may be unclear. Are they three sessions of one hour in duration? Or are they several sessions, each three hours long?

Em Dash

Use the em dash to set off a dependent clause that might be confusing with a comma:

> After the negotiation stalled, Carrie asked her client what stood in the way of saying yes—a technique she learned from 15 years in the manufacturing industry—and ultimately sealed the deal.

Em dashes can also be used to set information apart with emphasis:

> When he asked the client for feedback, Josh received a glowing compliment—an unexpected outcome given the number of complaints in the previous quarter.

En Dash

The en dash is longer than hyphen and shorter than an em dash. It connects values that are related or part of a range:

> The board approved the initiative with a 5-4 vote.

> Learn more about this topic on pages 16-19.

Parentheses

Use parentheses to set off information that shouldn't be emphasized:

> The team spent three consecutive days proofreading the recently completed documents (including purchasing analyses and quarterly reports).

If the statement is a complete sentence, put the period inside the parentheses:

> Shelly drove eight hours to attend the trade show. (She prefers driving to flying.)

Parenthetical text should immediately follow the reference:

> **Wrong:** Please research several dining options for Thursday's lunch with the regional managers (such as Italian, Chinese, or American).
> **Right:** Please research several dining options (such as Italian, Chinese, or American) for Thursday's lunch with the regional managers.

Apostrophe

Use an apostrophe to show possession:

> Margo's proposal was excellent, explaining every step and anticipating obstacles.

Insert an apostrophe in a word or between two words to take the place of letters that have been dropped:

> Jamal and Shelly don't *(do not)* understand the objectives.

Don't use an apostrophe if you're explaining that *it* possesses something:

> This company spent six months developing its mission statement.

Whether to use an apostrophe once or twice depends on joint versus separate possession: Two people (or things) can own something together or separately—which determines whether you use one or two apostrophes. For example, you would refer to *Jennifer and Ron's wedding* since both "own" the same wedding. But if you are referring to regional managers who submitted separate budget reports, you might say: *Please review Jennifer's and Ron's budget reports* (because each owns a separate report).

Follow Key Rules

Let's take a look at some of the time-tested grammar rules, most of which you might recall from English classes. While exceptions in grammar usage do exist, you should follow these rules to avoid confusing your reader or sounding unprofessional.

Make Sure Pronouns Agree With Nouns

A pronoun takes the place of a noun. Examples include subject pronouns (*I, he, she, we, they*), object pronouns (*me, him, her, us, them*), and relative pronouns (*who, whom*).

The most common distinction between pronouns is singular or plural. If the subject is singular, then the pronoun must be singular, and similarly for a plural subject:

> **Singular:** The newest branch manager was happy with *her* commission check.
> **Plural:** All three branch managers were happy with *their* commission checks.

When referring to a company, use the singular pronoun *its*:

> **Wrong:** After increasing market share by 40 percent in just one year, ZYC Corp. gave all *their* employees a generous bonus.
> **Right:** After increasing market share by 40 percent in just one year, ZYC Corp. gave all *its* employees a generous bonus.

While *their* may sound better, ZYC Corp. is singular and thus requires *its*, a singular pronoun.

Sometimes, matching up subjects and pronouns can be tricky.

> **Wrong:** The managing partner discussed several strategies to build the firm's forensic accounting practice, the one area that hasn't grown in the past year. *This* included a strong focus on social media marketing.
>
> **Right:** The managing partner discussed several strategies to build the firm's forensic accounting practice, the one area that hasn't grown in the past year. *These* included a strong focus on social media marketing.

While *this* may appear right, the correct pronoun is the plural *these*, which agrees with the plural noun *strategies* in the prior sentence.

One of the latest changes to grammar rules—which may help avoid a frequent error—is the approved use of *they* as a singular personal pronoun by the *Chicago Manual of Style* and the *Associated Press*. Here's an example:

> Tell the next candidate that they need to reschedule for next week.

Before the rule change, *he or she* would've been required instead of *they*.

In deciding between *I* or *me*, determine whether the pronoun is replacing a subject or an object within the sentence.

> **Wrong:** After meeting with the CFO, Suman told Pedro and *I* to begin ZY Partners' consulting report.
>
> **Right:** After meeting with the CFO, Suman told Pedro and *me* to begin ZY Partners' consulting report.

Suman is the subject and *Pedro and me* is the object. If you can't remember the subject-object rule, remove the other name (Pedro) and say it out loud: You'd say *Suman told me* (not *I*).

Here's another example:

> **Wrong:** I want to be sure that Larry, Carla, and *me* get to Denver by Tuesday afternoon.
>
> **Right:** I want to be sure that Larry, Carla, and *I* get to Denver by Tuesday afternoon.

Again, remove the other names and say it out loud: *I want to be sure that I* (not *me*) *get to Denver by Tuesday afternoon.*

One of the most difficult pronoun distinctions is who or whom. *Who* is the equivalent of *he* or *she*, whereas *whom* is the equivalent of *him* or *her*.

Here's an example where *who* is correct:

> **Wrong:** For the annual meeting, *whom* should be appointed team leader?
> **Right:** For the annual meeting, *who* should be appointed team leader?

As the equivalent of *he or she*, *who* is the proper pronoun, because you would say, *she* (not *her*) should be appointed team leader.

And here's an example where *whom* is correct:

> **Wrong:** The operations manager *who* I want to hire isn't available for the next three months.
> **Right:** The operations manager *whom* I want to hire isn't available for the next three months.

Referring to the operations manager, you would say, *I want him* or *I want her*, not *I want he* or *I want she*.

Another distinction is whether the subject is human, in which case the relative pronoun *who* is correct, or nonhuman, calling for *which* or *that*:

> **Wrong:** Laron was thrilled about the position with ZYS Industries, *who* offered him four weeks' vacation.
> **Right:** Laron was thrilled about the position with ZYS Industries, *which* offered him four weeks' vacation.

Make Sure Subjects Agree With Verbs

Singular subjects require singular verbs; plural subjects require plural verbs.

> **Wrong:** *There is* too many social media posts to read.
> **Right:** *There are* too many social media posts to read.

When choosing a singular or plural verb to agree in number with the subject of a sentence, disregard any phrases that follow the subject. The word immediately before the verb determines the number of the verb *only* if it's really the subject. Don't be fooled by how it sounds—double-check which word is the subject of the sentence. In the following examples, the subjects and verbs are in italics.

> **Wrong:** The *team* of customer service reps *are* committed to success.
> **Right:** The *team* of customer service reps *is* committed to success.

> **Wrong:** *Each* of the branch managers *agree* that work schedules should be more flexible.
> **Right:** *Each* of the branch managers *agrees* that work schedules should be more flexible.

> **Wrong:** The new cybersecurity *procedures*, which offer much-needed protection, *has been* difficult for most employees to learn.
> **Right:** The new cybersecurity *procedures*, which offer much-needed protection, *have been* difficult for most employees to learn.

Keep Tenses Consistent

Past, present, and future tenses are easily muddled in business writing. The goal is not to shift tenses in the flow of the sentence. Here are some sample pairs of sentences, one wrong and one right:

> **Shifted tense:** As soon as she *completed* the mobile analytics report, she *walked* out of the room and *takes* a taxi to the local pub to join her co-workers.
> **Consistent tense:** As soon as she *completed* the mobile analytics report, she *walked* out of the room and *took* a taxi to the local pub to join her co-workers.

> **Shifted tense:** If Steve *would pay* more attention to his direct reports, he *can be* an excellent manager.
> **Consistent tense:** If Steve *would pay* more attention to his direct reports, he *could be* an excellent manager.

> **Shifted tense:** Last year, the CEO *said* she *is* fed up with the accounting errors.
> **Consistent tense:** Last year, the CEO *said* she *was* fed up with the accounting errors.

Write Complete Sentences

Incomplete sentences, or sentence fragments, can sometimes be obvious, such as disguising phrases like "going to my next meeting" or "working on the last few pages of the report" as sentences. Others can be harder to spot.

A comma splice is when a comma has been used to join two independent clauses.

> Serena, the procurement manager, was born in Baltimore in 1972, it was far different then, before the Inner Harbor was developed.

We have three options to make this grammatically correct:

Make it two sentences: Serena, the procurement manager, was born in Baltimore in 1962. It was far different then, before the Inner Harbor was developed.

Use a semicolon: Serena, the procurement manager, was born in Baltimore in 1962; it was far different then, before the Inner Harbor was developed.

Add a prepositional phrase and commas: Serena, the procurement manager, was born in Baltimore in 1962 at a time when it was far different, before the Inner Harbor was developed.

Another common error is using *however* as a conjunction.

> The senior executives said that Gary's proposal was well written and compelling, however they agreed that many key details were omitted.

Again, we have three choices for constructing a complete sentence:

Create two sentences: The senior executives said that Gary's proposal was well written and compelling. However, they agreed that many key details were omitted.

Use a semicolon, and a comma after *however*: The senior executives said that Gary's proposal was well written and compelling; however, they agreed that many key details were omitted.

Replace *however* with *but*: The senior executives said that Gary's proposal was well written and compelling, but they agreed that many key details were omitted.

One last point: In some cases—as a reaction to another sentence—it's OK to use a sentence fragment for dramatic effect:

The marketing team has pledged to be more careful when recording figures. *Every last digit.*

What will it take for the southwest division to exceed its sales goals? *A lot more effort.*

The only caveat about sentence fragments: Use them sparingly.

Don't Dangle Your Participle

I don't like to use grammar-speak, but I've got to do it here. A participle is a word that has the features of both a verb and an adjective, and a phrase that includes a participle usually modifies a noun. A participial phrase is said to "dangle" when it's not located immediately before the noun it describes:

Wrong: Being an avid NASCAR fan, a ticket to the qualifying heat was a pleasant surprise for Andy.

Wrong: While driving to a business meeting, Megan's car overheated and she arrived an hour late.

See the problems? A ticket is not a NASCAR fan (Andy is), and Megan's car wasn't driving to the meeting (Megan was). The problem is that the descriptive phrase immediately precedes the wrong word. Let's correct those danglers:

Right: Being an avid NASCAR fan, Andy was pleasantly surprised with a ticket to the qualifying heat.

Right: While driving to a business meeting, Megan found that her car was overheating and she arrived an hour late.

You may find it easier to rewrite the sentence without the introductory modifying phrase, as in this example:

Right: Megan's car overheated on the way to the new business meeting, so she arrived an hour late.

Don't Leave Out *and* to Clarify Connections

Omitting the word *and* in a sentence where it would identify relationships among items is a common mistake. Here's an example:

Incorrect: We chose Santa Fe for its delightful climate, its large number of skilled workers, the local government's willingness to build roads, malls, and communication systems.

The conjunction *and* is needed to show that there are three reasons for the choice of Santa Fe. The missing *and* problem happens most often when you're enumerating a set of structurally parallel items (in the previous example, the reasons for choosing Santa Fe). To avoid the problem, begin by listing the items:

- delightful climate
- large number of skilled workers
- local government's willingness to build
  - roads
  - malls
  - communication systems.

With that list, you see there are three reasons (climate, workers, and willingness to build). The third reason has three items within it (roads, malls, and communication systems). When you know what your sentence includes, it's simple to write it clearly and accurately:

Correct: We chose Santa Fe for 1) its desirable location; 2) its large number of skilled workers; and 3) the local government's willingness to build roads, malls, and communication systems.

Don't Put Words or Phrases in the Wrong Positions

Never force the reader to guess at your meaning. See the following example and instructions for fixing it:

Confusing: Faye closed the deal with a real estate firm using an innovative approach to web marketing.

Who had the innovative approach to web marketing, Faye or the real estate firm? To clarify that Faye was the innovator, revise the sentence:

> **Clear:** Using an innovative approach to web marketing, Faye closed the deal with a real estate firm.

In the revised version, moving the phrase *using an innovative approach to web marketing* to the beginning of the sentence ties it directly to Faye.

In the next example, the phrase *last month* is poorly positioned. Did the sales team make the suggestion last month, or did they review the leads last month?

> **Confusing:** The sales team that was reviewing the most recent leads last month suggested that account reps target only prospects in Ohio and Indiana.
>
> **Clear:** After reviewing the most recent leads from last month, the sales team suggested that account reps target only prospects in Ohio and Indiana.

STEP 7 Break Some Old Rules

Regardless of what your English teachers may have told you back in grade school, high school, or college, it's OK to start a sentence with a conjunction or preposition like *and, or, but,* or *because.* These words can provide context for what you're about to write and can help you make a less abrupt transition from one sentence to another or from one paragraph to another. (If you still don't believe me, check out any newspaper or online news site.)

POINTER

It's OK to start sentences with *and, or, but,* and *because.*

Using certain conjunctions or prepositions to begin your sentence may enhance the natural rhythm of your words. Here are some examples:

> ***Because* to give context:** *Because* we've received so many customer complaints, I suggest a meeting on February 12 to review procedures for handling calls.

> **And to unify sentences:** Over the past 12 months, our company has been able to increase revenues while two of our major competitors have dropped out of the market. *And* we're poised to continue this success for the next five years.

Note that the two sentences in that example are too long to combine into one sentence joined by *and*. Beginning the second sentence with *and* carries the thought forward, while adding a dramatic pause.

> **But to contrast thoughts:** For a three-year period, online marketing had proven to be highly successful. In that time, we increased market share by 12 percent. Everyone, including the CFO, expected this trend to continue.
>
> *But* over the past two years, the number of new leads from online marketing has fallen off dramatically. The CFO said we need to shift strategies to appeal to mobile users.

Starting the second paragraph with *but over the past two years* provides a logical transition from the previous paragraph's discussion of the successful Internet marketing program.

Avoid Common Word Usage Errors

Beyond the cut-and-dry rules of grammar comes the issue of word choice. Perfect grammar surrounding the wrong word won't fix your mistake. Often, the errors occur because different words are spelled similarly. In other cases, it's simply a matter of not knowing the correct meaning of words you're trying to use. (See Appendix C for a list of commonly misused words and examples of correct usage.) A couple of them deserve a more detailed explanation here:

Affect vs. Effect

You can diminish the confusion between these two by recognizing that, in most common uses, *affect* is a verb and *effect* is a noun.

> **Wrong:** Poor morale negatively *effects* the bottom line.
> **Right:** Poor morale negatively *affects* the bottom line.
>
> **Wrong:** Poor morale can have a devastating *affect* on the bottom line.

STEP 7

Right: Poor morale can have a devastating *effect* on the bottom line.

There are, however, two occasions when affect and effect change places. *Affect* becomes a noun when describing a person's visible emotion:

> The psychiatrist observed his *affect* during the cognitive tests.

Effect becomes a verb when it means "bring about":

> With her policies, the new CEO hoped to *effect* meaningful change in the company.

Those less-common uses of affect and effect seldom occur in business text, but it's good to be prepared.

i.e. vs. e.g.

If you mean "for example," use *e.g.* Use *i.e.* only if you mean "in other words" or "that is." These abbreviations have come to English from Latin: *e.g.* is the shortened form of exempli gratia and *i.e.* is the shortened form of id est. Both are common in business communication and used most often in parenthetical text. Be sure to insert a comma after the second period in each of these abbreviations.

Here are two examples of incorrect and proper usage:

> **Wrong:** Carmen prefers brochures with bright colors (*i.e.*, orange, red, and green).
> **Right:** Carmen prefers brochures with bright colors (*e.g.*, orange, red, and green).
>
> **Wrong:** Your blog posts should be short (*e.g.*, 200 words or less).
> **Right:** Your blog posts should be short (*i.e.*, 200 words or less).

Your Turn

Improving your grammar takes practice and the patience to look up the right usage on a website or in a resource book. Though nobody expects you to be perfect, you should avoid mistakes that could make you appear sloppy, lazy, or uneducated. The following exercises will give you some quick practice in correcting common grammatical mistakes. You'll find the correct answers at the end of the chapter.

1. Circle the correct word for noun–pronoun agreement or verb–subject agreement:

   a. The team of supervisors always **exceed, exceeds** expectations.

   b. Each of the regional managers **agree, agrees** that service has improved.

   c. We believe in XR Company and **its, their** people.

   d. The new cybersecurity precautions, which could offer much-needed peace of mind, **has, have** met with strong opposition.

   e. Athos, along with four of his co-workers, **exercise, exercises** every evening after work.

   f. Seth and three of his co-workers **exercise, exercises** every morning before work.

2. Circle the word with the apostrophe in the correct position:

   a. The daycare manager misplaced the **children's, childrens'** favorite toys.

   b. Maria lost all the data on her laptop computer when **its, it's** hard drive crashed.

   c. The **supervisor's, supervisors'** best asset is his technical knowledge.

   d. The head of operations, **whose, who's** subordinates work hard, earned another production award.

e. **It's, Its** hard to keep morale strong during a corporate upheaval.

f. Please review both proposals—**Joan's and Shing's, Joan and Shing's**—by June 8.

3. Circle the correct abbreviation—i.e. or e.g.

a. Bring back the old peer review systems (**i.e., e.g.,** managers from each division critiquing one another's performance).

b. For the European conference, consider some new destinations (**i.e., e.g.,** Brussels, Nice, and Seville).

c. The new finance director demands near-perfect quarterly reports (**i.e., e.g.,** no typos).

d. If you go to Italy, be sure to sample many different dishes (**i.e., e.g.,** lasagna, risotto, and tortellini).

The Next Step

Writing concise, well-organized, and compelling emails and documents—with correct grammar—enables you to achieve better results. But writing error-free text the first time is rare. To ensure that your message comes out the way you want it to, you'll need to carefully review your text. We'll address that in Step 8 (Edit and Proofread Effectively).

Your Turn Answers

- 1a: exceeds, 1b: agrees, 1c: its, 1d: have, 1e: exercises, 1f: exercise
- 2a: children's, 2b: its, 2c: supervisor's, 2d: whose, 2e: It's, 2f: Joan's and Shing's
- 3a: i.e., 3b: e.g., 3c: i.e., 3d: e.g.

Step 8

Edit and Proofread Effectively

Overview

- Learn editing and proofreading best practices.
- Follow the three-stage editing process—message, organization, and mechanics.
- See how editing can dramatically improve documents.

If I had a magic formula for perfect editing and proofreading, I'd gladly share it with you. And don't expect spell check or some other software to protect you from all errors. They're far from infallible, although they can be a valuable part of the editing process. Even newspapers with professional editors and proofreaders aren't immune to faux-pas, especially with the pressure to deliver content 24/7.

While your text can't always be 100 percent error-free, take every precaution to avoid mistakes, especially the obvious ones. Like poor grammar, sloppy proofreading can make you come across as lazy and unprofessional.

Let's first distinguish between editing and proofreading. Editing involves rereading to ensure that your text is clear, well organized, and in the appropriate style, among other standards. Proofreading helps you catch errors in spelling and punctuation, incorrect words, and other grammar mistakes. While editing typically precedes proof-ing, the two often overlap, so we'll treat them as part of a single technique in explaining best practices and the key stages. We won't look at the specific editorial changes you may want to make in your text (covered in earlier steps), but we'll examine examples of editing and proofreading in action.

Don't Write and Edit at the Same Time

When starting to write, let your words pour out as quickly as they come into your head so you don't interrupt the flow of ideas (see freewriting in Step 1 and rhythm in Step 3). If you stop after every sentence or paragraph to edit what you've just jotted down, you'll exhaust yourself in switching back and forth from writer to reader. By getting text onscreen (or on paper if you're old fashioned) as rapidly as you can, you allot more time for the crucial editing and proofreading phase—and in the long run may save yourself time.

Once you've completed the first draft, let another person edit and proofread your work if possible. But if you need to go solo, let some time pass—30 to 60 minutes or until the next day if possible—before you start the editing and proofing process. This way you won't get too attached to your words, and you can refocus your concentration and review the text with a fresh pair of eyes. Taking this break will also help you read from the recipient's point of view.

POINTER

If you want to write better, know what will *read* better to others.

To become an effective editor and proofreader, you need to be that reader and answer key ques-tions about the text: Can I follow the key points? Did the writer convince me to support their posi-tion or lead me to take the requested action? Are there any wasted words? Does the text flow logi-cally from start to finish? And don't forget your gut instinct: Is it good?

Review Tool 8-1 for a list of best practices and select the ones that fit your needs. Over time, you'll discover the combination of tech-niques that works best.

Tool 8-1
Editing and Proofreading Best Practices

Read Aloud
Read your text out loud in a staccato, syllable-by-syllable rhythm so you can hear the errors. For example, when sounding out, "Heather outlined four new web marketing strategies is her report," you'll probably notice that *is* should be *in* (an error that many spell-check functions wouldn't catch).

Read Backward
By reading backward, you'll force yourself to review one word at a time instead of getting mesmerized by the flow of sentences and paragraphs.

Review Each Sentence as a Separate Entity
Look at each sentence as a separate message, which will also help you avoid being mesmerized by the flow of ideas.

Be Consistent in Style
Even if your organization doesn't have a style guide, maintain consistency within each document when making these choices:
- capitalization
- full names, first names, or last names
- abbreviations, such as using *search engine optimization (SEO)* the first time and then *SEO* for subsequent mentions
- numerals or numbers spelled out
- indication of time, for example 2:00 p.m. versus 2 p.m.
- spacing
- use of graphical elements, such as bold, italic, underlining, font size, and color.

Compose and Edit Emails in Word
Compose and edit important emails and text messages in Word or a similar program, where you can more easily use graphical tools (such as different fonts and sizes, spacing, bullets, and numbers) and spell-check functions. Then, when you're satisfied, copy and paste the text into an email. This will also help you avoid potential disasters like accidentally hitting send!

STEP 8

Use Track Changes or a Similar Application

Take advantage of the tracking feature of your word-processing program, which should enable you to view in different modes: final with markup, final without markup, original with markup, and original without markup.

Print It Out

Print out an important email or document, perhaps in larger type. The average person is more likely to catch errors on a piece of paper than on a screen. But use discretion (you don't need to print out a two-sentence email) to help protect the environment.

Follow the Three-Stage Process

Editing and proofreading can be divided into three major focus areas: message, organization, and mechanics. Each area is addressed separately because it's impossible to pay close attention to all three at the same time. Let's look at these stages.

Message

Editing should begin with the message because it makes no sense to waste time reorganizing or reviewing the mechanics of text that isn't conveying your points clearly. To review the clarity of your message, ask yourself a few simple questions. These are similar to the ones you asked when you started writing the document (see Step 1):

- Is the purpose or bottom line clear?
- Is the action required of the reader clear?
- Are the other important points clear?
- Is the tone appropriate for the message?
- Is the message written in a positive rather than negative way?

As you answer these questions, mark any text you're not satisfied with, such as a confusing action step. Onscreen, use the highlighting feature or put that block of text in a different color. On paper, circle or highlight a group of words or sentences that may need revision. Then work on clarifying your message in each of the places you've marked.

STEP 8

POINTER

Editing is a three-stage process that focuses separately on message, organization, and mechanics.

Organization

Everything you write—from lengthy documents to brief emails and text messages—needs to be organized so that the reader can see where you're going and then follow you to the end. This second stage of editing takes a hard look at how well you've imposed a logical order on what you're trying to say.

Here are some questions to ask yourself to determine if your text is properly organized:

- Is information separated into small chunks that are easy to process?
- Are those chunks arranged in a logical sequence?
- Does each paragraph contain just one basic idea so readers won't get confused?
- Are there transitions unifying sentences, paragraphs, and sections to help ideas flow smoothly from start to finish?
- Is the structure reasonably similar throughout different sections?

One method to separate and arrange your ideas is to read your text and list all the key points conveyed. In essence, you're reoutlining it. This can be much easier when you're looking at text you've written than when you're staring at a blank screen or page. Reoutlining also helps identify any important concepts you may have omitted. You can list them at the bottom of the page, or on a separate page and incorporate them as you reorganize the text. You'll also be able to spot repeated or similar ideas scattered throughout and then merge them into a single paragraph or section.

If you developed an initial outline before you started your first draft, compare that version to the reoutline to see if you omitted anything you initially intended to include. During this stage, you may decide to change the order in which the ideas are presented so they flow more logically from one to the next.

Consider adding subheads or a few words before each section (set in bold or italic or underlined—or a combination of these) to pinpoint the key message that follows and to further separate each concept. (See Step 4 for more discussion of subheads.)

STEP 8

Some aspects of good organization are more subjective than the message and proper mechanics, and may depend on your personal style or the reader's preference. For example, the same information can be effectively conveyed through shorter or longer paragraphs. And you can explain a multifaceted concept by using bullets to list the facets or by writing a few traditional paragraphs with no bulleted items.

When you get comfortable with your own method of organizing, you'll find that it not only promotes readability, but also simplifies your writing process, because you can move text around into separate categories more quickly and confidently.

Mechanics

Most of the grunt work comes in the third stage: reviewing the mechanics of your text (which can also be considered proofreading). Mechanics form the microlevel of the document, not the macro message or the midlevel organization. It's the nitty gritty of editing.

Reviewing spelling, punctuation, grammar, and word usage may require you to be in a different frame of mind than you are when evaluating message clarity and organization. You need to scrutinize individual words or groups of words instead of the entire text. Here are some questions you need to ask:

- Typos and Punctuation
    - Are any words misspelled?
    - Are any incorrect homonyms (soundalikes such as there and their) used?
    - Are any words missing or out of place in a sentence?
    - Have you placed apostrophes correctly?
    - Are all proper names spelled correctly?
    - Do all your sentences end with the appropriate punctuation?
    - Are all commas and periods placed inside quotation marks?
- Grammar and Syntax
    - Do subjects and verbs agree in number?

- Do nouns and pronouns agree in number?
- Is the text written in a consistent tense?
- Are sentences written in a parallel structure?
- Are bulleted or numbered lists written in a parallel structure?
- Does each introductory phrase directly relate to the noun that immediately follows it?
- Is all text written in complete sentences, where appropriate?
- Are there short, choppy sentences that can be combined for better flow?

- Word Usage
  - Is there any stuffy language that can be replaced with simpler words?
  - Are there any weak, passive verbs that can be replaced with more powerful, active verbs?
  - Can you eliminate any redundant language?
  - Is there jargon or "business-speak" that can be simplified with more widely understood terminology?

Start with the available spelling- and grammar-checking feature, which helps catch obvious mistakes—but don't depend on it. Despite advances in language usage, spell check may not catch every homonym you've used incorrectly (*here, hear; do, due; there, their, they're*). And as for the grammar-checking feature, sometimes the software's suggestions are just plain wrong.

Examples of Editing in Action

Editing your own text can be a challenging and painstaking process. I wish I could sit with you and make specific suggestions as you do it. The second-best option is for you to look at several first-draft documents and evaluate their message, organization, and mechanics and examine how to improve each aspect.

What follows are three documents (which all could be within the text of an email): a meeting review, an explanation of the company purchasing policy, and a blog post. Some of the documents may need corrections in one or two of the focus areas of message, organization, and mechanics; others may need changes in all three areas.

You'll find the rough-draft versions of each document first, followed by an evaluation of the message, the organization, and the mechanics. Because the evaluations are brief and general, you'll gain most from studying the text in "tracked" format—that is, with deletions, additions, and changes showing. In this format, you'll be able to see exactly what was replaced or inserted with a degree of detail that the evaluations don't offer. The tracked and final versions of each document are shown after each evaluation.

Meeting Review

Rough Draft

Sarah,

This email is to review and confirm what we discussed at the meeting yesterday morning from 9 to 11 a.m. In that meeting, we talked about the fact that your staff of employees needs to provide assistance to my team with the different facets of the execution of the direct mail campaign.

Below, I have listed the important next steps, which are bulleted, that need to be followed by your staff:

- Assuming responsibility for the phone calls to the sources you have in order to be able to build a complete and comprehensive database.
- Conducting meetings among your staff and my team in which all personnel present would gain an understanding of what each is responsible for during this entire process.
- Handling each and every incidence of complaining by the various customers, many of whom may be displeased with the level and quality of customer service they receive.
- How the execution of the database marketing program will proceed, including how much it will cost, what we

expect the revenues to be and what type of follow-up we should consider implementing.

I have all the confidence in the world that both of our teams will work well together to complete all that we need to do and be in a great position to produce an effective direct mail campaign with a lower cost.

Should there be any questions, concerns, or items that you feel should be clarified, please don't hesitate to pick up the phone and call me. Or, if you prefer, you can email me directly.

Sincerely,
Sean

Evaluation

- Message: OK
- Organization: OK
- Mechanics:
    ◦ weak, passive verbs
    ◦ stuffy language, wordiness
    ◦ redundancies
    ◦ nonparallel structure in bulleted items.

Editing, in Tracked Format

Sarah,

~~This email is to review and confirm what we discussed at the meeting.~~ <u>Following</u> yesterday<u>'s</u> ~~morning from 9 to 11 a.m. In that~~ meeting <u>on</u> ~~we talked about the fact that your staff of employees needs to provide assistance to my team with the different facets of the execution of~~ the direct mail campaign<u>,</u> <u>here's</u> ~~Below, I have listed the important~~ <u>a review of the</u> next steps~~, which are bulleted, that need to be followed by~~ <u>for</u> your staff:

- <u>Call your</u> ~~Assuming responsibility for the phone calls to the~~ sources <u>to help</u> ~~you have in order to be able to~~ build a ~~complete and~~ comprehensive database.

- Conduct~~ing~~ meetings <u>with both of our teams to discuss responsibilities.</u> ~~among your staff and my team in which all personnel present would gain an understanding of what each is responsible for during this entire process.~~
- Handl<u>e customer complaints.</u> ~~ing each and every incidence of complaining by the various customers, many of whom may be displeased with the level and quality of customer service they receive.~~
- <u>Determine costs and anticipated revenues.</u> ~~How the execution of the database marketing program will proceed, including how much it will cost, what we expect the revenues to be and what type of follow-up we should consider implementing.~~

<u>I'm confident that</u> ~~I have all the confidence in the world that both of~~ our teams will work well together to ~~complete all that we need to do and be in a great position to~~ produce an effective direct mail campaign <u>at</u> ~~with~~ a lower cost.

<u>Please call or email me if you have</u> ~~Should there be~~ any questions.<u>_</u> ~~, concerns, or items that you feel should be clarified, please don't hesitate to pick up the phone and call me. Or, if you prefer, you can email me directly.~~

Sincerely,
Sean

Final Document

Sarah,

Following yesterday's meeting on the direct mail campaign, here's a review of the next steps for your staff:
- Call your sources to help build a comprehensive database.
- Conduct meetings with both of our teams to discuss responsibilities.
- Handle customer complaints.
- Determine costs and anticipated revenues.

I'm confident that our teams will work well together to produce an effective direct mail campaign at a lower cost.

Please call or email me if you have any questions.

Sincerely,
Sean

Explanation of Company Purchasing Policy

Rough Draft

So we can do a better job in handling our claims with regard to materials purchased at the MNO or XYZ stores, we are requesting all contractors to use the supply report for those particular stores. When you use our firm's accounts for these stores, please be absolutely sure that you make a complete purchase for the job at one time. Every time you make a purchase, the store is generating an invoice. As a result, more work is created not only for us, but for you as well.

An example of this occurred when one contractor went to the XYZ store five times in one week for the same claim. Each purchase was for very minor items. This takes time out of your employee's production and project efficiency, as well as costing our firm and you more money for that particular claim.

We've heard many contractors who complain that it takes longer for their employees to relocate the materials at the stores, and this may be the reason why. It's my recommendation that you and your subcontractors email all of the orders in to MNO store or XYZ store at least 24 hours prior to the pickup time. Please make sure that you order the materials necessary for a repair job, and have them put it on one invoice. By doing this, we should minimize your employees' and subcontractors' down time, travel time, and reduce operating expense for you and our company.

In addition, make certain that you use the correct purchase order number, not the customer's phone number or social security number. If you do not use the correct purchase order number, you will be advised to go the website of either of the appropriate stores and make all of the corrections for each claim. This needs to be done. For those of you who continue to have problems with getting the correct purchase order number on the invoices, I will have to take you out of the rotation until this can be corrected.

Evaluation

- Message: Fairly clear—procedures for purchases at these stores
- Organization: Good
- Mechanics:
  - misspelled words
  - redundancies
  - words missing
  - vague use of pronouns, such as this and that, with no clear noun reference
  - weak, passive verbs
  - lack of number agreement between subject and verb
  - stuffy language, wordiness
  - inaccurate capitalization
  - inaccurate use of apostrophe
  - phrases and sentences without parallel structure
  - dangling participle.

Editing, in Tracked Format

To ~~So we can do a~~ better ~~job in handling our~~ handle claims for ~~with regard to~~ materials purchased at the MNO or XYZ stores, ~~we are requesting all~~ contractors should ~~to~~ use the supply report for those particular stores. ~~When you use our firm's accounts for these stores, please b~~Be absolutely sure to ~~that you make a complete~~ purchase everything you need for the job at one time. ~~Every time you make a purchase,~~ Otherwise, the store ~~is~~ generates ~~ing~~ multiple ~~an~~ invoices for each purchase, resulting in unnecessary work for both of us. ~~As a result, more work is created not only for us, but for you as well.~~

For ~~An~~ example, ~~of this occurred when~~ one contractor went to ~~the~~ XYZ store five times in one week for the same claim, each time ~~Each purchase was~~ for ~~very~~ minor items. This duplication of effort costs employees valuable production time, and ~~takes time out of your employee's production and~~

~~project efficiency, as well as~~ cost<u>s</u> ~~ing our firm~~ <u>the stores</u> ~~and you more money for that particular claim~~ <u>time and money to produce the extra paperwork.</u>

~~We've heard many contractors who complain that it takes longer for their employees to relocate the materials at the stores, and this may be the reason why. It's my~~ <u>I</u> recommenda~~tion~~ that you and your subcontractors email all ~~of the~~ orders ~~in~~ to MNO store or XYZ store at least 24 hours prior to the pickup time<u>, and be</u> ~~Please make~~ sure that <u>all</u> ~~you order the~~ materials <u>needed for a job are</u> ~~necessary for a repair job, and have them put it~~ <u>listed</u> on one invoice. ~~By doing this, we~~ <u>Doing so</u> should ~~minimize your employees' and subcontractors' down time, travel time, and~~ reduce operating expense<u>s</u> for <u>all parties.</u> ~~you and our company.~~

In addition, <u>remember to submit</u> ~~make certain that you use~~ the correct purchase order number, not the customer's phone number or social security number. ~~If you do not use the correct purchase order number,~~ <u>If not,</u> you will be <u>forced</u> ~~advised~~ to go <u>to</u> the website of either ~~of the appropriate~~ store<u>s</u> and ~~make all of the~~ correct ~~ions for~~ each claim. ~~This needs to be done. For:~~ <u>T</u>hose of you who continue to <u>submit the wrong</u> ~~have problems with getting the correct purchase order~~ number<u>s</u> on the invoices<u>,</u> ~~I~~ will <u>be</u> ~~have to~~ take<u>n</u> ~~you~~ out of the rotation until this <u>error</u> can be corrected.

Final Document

To better handle claims for materials purchased at the MNO or XYZ stores, contractors should use the supply report for those particular stores. Be sure to purchase everything you need for the job at one time. Otherwise, the store generates multiple invoices for each purchase, resulting in unnecessary work for both of us.

For example, one contractor went to XYZ store five times in one week for the same claim, each time for minor items. This duplication of effort costs employees valuable production time, and costs the stores time and money to produce the extra paperwork.

I recommend that you and your subcontractors email all orders to MNO store or XYZ store at least 24 hours prior to the pickup time, and be sure that all materials needed for a job are listed on one invoice. Doing so should reduce operating expenses for all parties.

In addition, remember to submit the correct purchase order number, not the customer's phone number or social security number. If not, you will be forced to go to the website of either store and correct each claim. Those of you who continue to submit the wrong numbers on the invoices will be taken out of the rotation until this error can be corrected.

Blog Post

Rough Draft

With stories, the earlier they're introduced into a speech the better. This way, one is able to create engagement from people right from the start. I recently attended a seminar in Manhattan where I, as an attendee, heard the speaker open by saying how happy he—an ex New Yorker—was to be back in the city where he came from and was now able to indulge in New York bagels. The audience immediately, from the start, felt a greater sense of connection!

Everyone loves to be the recipient of good storytelling. This difference could be between putting your audience to sleep or being able to wow them with a memorable message.

What's also important is tailoring your story to the requirements of the audience. What moves this audience? What are this audience's day-to-day challenges? What is this audience's long-term goals? Don't simply add a random story—relate it to your message. By sharing experiences that they're more likely to care about, you'll add personal meaning and make your stories more relevant.

Relate the story to your message instead of plugging in a random story. One example is if you're speaking about effectively hiring to a group of small employers. In this specific case, you might share a story about a colleague who used a really offbeat technique to recruit someone who turned out to be her most valuable employee.

Want to learn more? Check in with us again next week when we'll provide three more simple tips for incorporating storytelling into your public speaking.

Evaluation

- Message: Clear—storytelling can help speakers connect with their audiences.
- Organization: Poor. The blog post opened with a statement that stories should be introduced early in a presentation to engage the audience, leading the reader to believe more discussion on this theme would follow. But then the second paragraph shifted to a more general point of how speakers can effectively use storytelling. The third paragraph mixed up two distinct (albeit similar) suggestions—tailoring the story to the audience and relating the story to your message.
- Mechanics:
  - redundancies
  - wordiness
  - repetitive language
  - weak nouns that could be turned into strong verbs
  - shifted tenses (singular and plural)
  - errors in subject–verb and noun–pronoun agreement
  - typos (wrong words) that spell check won't catch.

To revise this blog post, start by reorganizing the information into a logical order:

- First, open with a clear theme: *why storytelling is an effective tool for speeches.*
- Then list and number the three tips for incorporating stories into speeches:
  - Introduce the story early in the presentation.
  - Tailor the story to your audience.
  - Relate the story to your message.
- After your opening, lead into these suggestions: *Here are three tips for integrating stories into your next speech.*

STEP
8

Editing, in Tracked Format

Everyone loves a good story. Incorporating storytelling into your public speaking can make the difference between putting your audience to sleep or wowing them with a memorable message.

Here are three tips for integrating stories into your next speech:

1. Introduce the story early in your speech ~~With stories, the earlier they're introduced into a speech the better. This way, one is able~~ to ~~create~~ engage ~~ment from~~ people ~~right~~ from the start. I recently attended a seminar in Manhattan where ~~I, as an attendee, heard~~ the speaker open~~ed~~ by saying how happy he—an ex-New Yorker—was to be back in the city ~~where he came from and was now able to~~ so he could indulge in New York bagels. The audience immediately—~~from the start,~~ felt ~~a greater sense of~~ more connect~~ed~~! ~~ion!~~

~~Everyone loves to be the recipient of good storytelling. This difference could be between putting your audience to sleep or being able to wow them with a memorable message.~~

~~What's also important is tailoring~~ 2. Tailor your story to the ~~requirements of the~~ audience. What moves this ~~audience~~ group of people? What are ~~this audience's~~ their day-to-day challenges? What ~~is this audience's~~ are their long-term goals? ~~Don't simply add a random story; relate it to your message.~~ By sharing experiences that they're more likely to care about, you'll add personal meaning and make your stories more relevant.

3. Relate the story to your message instead of just plugging in a random story. ~~One example is~~ For example, if you're speaking about effective~~ly~~ hiring to a group of small employers, ~~In this specific case,~~ you might talk ~~share a story~~ about a colleague who used ~~a really~~ an extremely offbeat technique to recruit someone who turned out to be her most valuable employee.

Want to learn more? Check in with us ~~again~~ next week, when we'll provide three more simple tips for incorporating storytelling into your public speaking.

Final Document

Everyone loves a good story. Incorporating storytelling into your public speaking can make the difference between putting your audience to sleep or wowing them with a memorable message.

Here are three tips for integrating stories into your next speech:

1. Introduce the story early in your speech to engage people from the start. I recently attended a seminar in Manhattan where the speaker opened by saying how happy he—an ex–New Yorker—was to be back in the city so he could indulge in New York bagels. The audience immediately felt more connected!

2. Tailor your story to the audience. What moves this group of people? What are their day-to-day challenges? What are their long-term goals? By sharing experiences that they're more likely to care about, you'll add personal meaning and make your stories more relevant.

3. Relate the story to your message instead of just plugging in a random story. For example, if you're speaking about effective hiring to a group of small employers, you might talk about a colleague who used an extremely offbeat technique to recruit someone who turned out to be her most valuable employee.

Want to learn more? Check in with us next week, when we'll provide three more simple tips for incorporating storytelling into your public speaking.

(Blog post example courtesy of Jayne Latz, president of Corporate Speech Solutions.)

Your Turn

Editing requires a meticulous review of your document's message (clarity of content), organization (logical structure and flow), and mechanics (punctuation, spelling, grammar, and word usage). Try these exercises:

1. Find the word-usage errors:

> The principle reason for Grayson's disappointment is that nobody on the team complemented him on the keynote speech he delivered at the annual meeting.

2. Find the typo:

> Be extra careful when you review all the exercises in this section. Look closely and see if you can find the the mistake, which is often difficult to spot.

3. Revise the following document using these guidelines:
   - Delete unnecessary words.
   - Use simple words and parallel structure.
   - Ensure that verbs and subjects agree in number.
   - Make verb tense consistent throughout.
   - Fix spelling, punctuation, grammar, or usage mistakes.
   - If desired, insert subheads and bullets to improve organization.

> Dan,
>
> Everyone in our division believes strongly in the need for accuracy in shipping. We take it seriously and consider its the part our business that distinguish us from the rest of the competition. Mistakes on orders can be heavily damaging to the company.
>
> Too many errors have occurred on shipments. It has come to my attention that shipment errors have gone up 2 15 percent over the time period covering the past nine months. It is my opinion that this is probably a result of outdated technology. Thus the only, solution is to make the investment in the latest, state-of-the-art shipping technology. This technology will be so much better for all partys involved.
>
> Nobody likes sloppy work by any one or group. After my observations, I have concluded that a good many of the shipping clerks do work that many, including I, consider sloppy. No way can this be tolerated any more. The entire

department needs to undergo training on proper procedures. This training can be handled by PXX Partners, experts
in this type of training.

We have also notice a large number of safety violations, that
can be dangerous if they're not corrected. So let's get on it.
I want those violations to be corrected within a four-month
time period. The best ones to handle this is RLS Risk Services,
a prominent risk management firm. Let's get on this.

Regards,
Gail

The Next Step

While careful editing and proofreading are essential for longer documents such as reports and proposals, they're also crucial for emails
and texts. We'll take a closer look at how to compose these messages
effectively in Step 9 (Master Emails and Electronic Communication).

Answers to Your Turn questions 1 and 2:

- Change *principle* to *principal* and *complemented* to
  complimented.
- Delete the extra *the*.

Step 9

Master Emails and Electronic Communication

Overview

- Enhance email efficiency.
- Craft explicit, action-generating subject lines.
- Follow email etiquette.
- Compose mobile-friendly emails and professional text messages.

How did we ever manage without email? Some of us remember the last century when we mailed letters, sent faxes, and left lots of voicemails. Today, email rules as the number one business communication method, despite the explosion of social media (see Step 10) and other new channels that continue to emerge.

Email is an amazing tool. Well-constructed email messages can provide clear directions that promote efficiency, build morale, solidify key relationships, generate leads, and offer many other benefits. But emails can also cause problems that didn't exist in the pre-Internet era. It's the ultimate double-edged sword—and we all have our share of horror stories, including emails that were sent to the wrong person or shouldn't have been sent at all. And you've undoubtedly been on the receiving end of nasty or condescending emails that make you want to punch the screen or throw your mobile device against the wall!

Plus, email is an enormous time waster. A study by *Inc.* revealed that the average U.S. worker spent six hours a day checking emails (James 2015). Are you kidding me? How do organizations get anything done? And the number of emails continues to skyrocket, about 120 per day per person in the latest count—thanks in part to mobile devices that allow us to easily send emails 24/7, according to the Radicati Group (2015). The more emails we send, the more replies we receive—and the more precious time we spend processing them. Every five emails sent generate an average of three replies; eliminating one out of every five emails would cut the number of incoming emails by 12 percent and free up our time for other tasks (Song, Halsey, and Burress 2007).

This step will explain the most important practices for maximizing efficiency with emails and other electronic communication tools.

Reduce the Number of Emails

Given the startling amount of time spent on electronic communication in the workplace, everyone should strive to become more efficient with emails. Still, some of the strategies that follow may need to be adjusted based on the culture of your organization, as well as the preference of your supervisor, client, and other readers.

Don't Always Reply All

We all receive emails that we couldn't care less about. Let's say the purchasing administrator emails 15 team leaders asking what supplies they need. By force of habit, 12 of them hit reply all, filling everyone's inboxes with every detail. Does every other team leader need to know that Maria needs two boxes of copy paper, 75 three-ring binders, and a dozen staple removers?

While you can't control others' email habits, you can help unclog co-workers' inboxes by not hitting reply all unless necessary. And when requesting information from many colleagues, consider asking them to "reply to me only."

See what happens when everyone continues to cc everyone in the original email chain:

Email String

1. From Suman to Jennifer (cc Carlos)
Carlos and I are in the process of modifying ABC Industries' cybersecurity plan and we need the one-page technical guidelines you developed last year.

2. From Jennifer to Suman and Carlos
Please see the attached guidelines and keep me posted on how the project is going or if you have technical issues.

3. From Carlos to Jennifer (cc Suman)
Thanks very much, Jennifer.

4. From Carlos to Suman (cc Jennifer)
I'll revise the text and incorporate the technical specs from Jennifer's guidelines.

5. From Suman to Carlos (cc Jennifer)
Perfect, Carlos. I'll await your revisions. Meanwhile, I'll schedule a date when you and I can meet with Julie at ABC to show her the new plan.

6. From Carlos to Suman (cc Jennifer)
That sounds good, Suman. Please make it Wednesday or Thursday in one of the next two weeks.

7. From Suman to Carlos (cc Jennifer)
No problem, Carlos. Those days should work for me too.

After email 3 (Carlos thanks Jennifer for her assistance), Jennifer no longer needs to be copied. Emails 4 to 7, dealing with drafting the cybersecurity plan and arranging a meeting with Julie at ABC Industries, don't involve Jennifer. So by copying her on those four emails, Suman and Carlos are clogging up Jennifer's inbox and wasting her time.

A better approach: Suman and Carlos should wait until the new cybersecurity plan is approved by ABC Industries (assuming no technical problems requiring Jennifer's assistance) and then email Jennifer a brief update about the client's reaction, while thanking her for her support.

Don't Acknowledge Every Email

In your effort to be courteous, you may be wasting your time—and the reader's time. Check out this all-too-common exchange between two colleagues, even when they work on the same floor:

> **Andre:** I misplaced your suggestions for the status update that you emailed last week. Please resend.
> **Mia:** See the requested suggestions below.
> **Andre:** Thanks, Mia.
> **Mia:** No problem.

While few would disagree that Mia's "No problem" wasn't necessary, Andre's "Thanks, Mia" was also a waste of time. I'm not telling you to be rude; just differentiate between a useful reply and a needless "thank you." As long-time colleagues, Andre and Mia shouldn't waste their time on trivial acknowledgments. But if you're the devil's advocate, you may ask what the big deal is. It takes less than 30 seconds to read and delete the email, right? Yes, but those half-minutes can quickly turn into hours of unproductive time.

Use discretion before sending that acknowledgment. Consider the topic, time sensitivity, and the sender's expectations.

Avoid Instinctive "I'll Get Back to You" Replies

Many individuals are conditioned to respond immediately to nearly every email, to notify the sender that they received it and are working on getting the required information. That's another time-waster—which I'm guilty of frequently, including a few years ago, while replying to an affiliate with whom I had been working for three years:

> **Brian (September 20, 11 a.m.):** I need your vehicle information for our October 10 presentation at YXZ Company. Please email it to me by September 25.
> **Jack (September 20, 12:30 p.m.):** I'm tied up in a workshop all day so I'll email this to you as soon as I can.

> **Jack (September 21, 9:30 a.m.):** Below is my vehicle information that you requested.

Soon after I sent my September 20 email, I realized how unnecessary it was. The next morning, I sent Brian the requested information, four days ahead of his deadline. In most cases, you don't need to update the person that you will take care of their request later; just wait until you're finished and send it.

Do some individuals want an immediate response for every email to make sure you've received it? Sure, so identify them and try not to send unnecessary replies to those who don't need them. Again, it goes back to your organization's culture and the sender's preferences.

Know When to—and When Not to—Email

An email (or text) is not always the most efficient way to communicate. Still, many of us get caught in a string of emails that ends up wasting everyone's time. See the following email conversation between two co-workers from different offices looking to set up a conference call:

> **May 5—Alison (Houston office):** I suggest we set up a call with the Houston and Atlanta supervisors during the week of June 20 to discuss changes in the corporate advisory practice. What day and time would work on your end?
> **May 6—Ramón (Atlanta office):** I don't know. Our managers have told me that they don't believe these calls are very productive.
> **May 7—Alison:** I'm aware that they weren't happy with prior calls, so we've prepared a detailed agenda.
> **May 8—Ramón:** The other issue with previous calls, according to our managers, was the lack of follow-up.
> **May 9—Alison:** Are they talking about weekly or biweekly updates, follow-up phone calls, or other issues?

Five emails and several days later, Alison and Ramón still haven't scheduled the call. Both neglected a critical business tool—the telephone! Had one of them called the other, the meeting could've been scheduled in two minutes. Then, Alison or Ramón could've sent a brief email documenting the agreed-upon details.

If you find yourself in the middle of a useless email string, pick up the phone! You could save a lot of time on both ends. For those in organizations that use Outlook Invite or other calendar programs, follow the protocol for arranging meetings—but don't waste time on an email string to nowhere.

Write More Productive Emails

To further boost productivity, construct concise and explicit emails that make it easier for the other person to reply and help you work more efficiently.

Be Explicit About What You Want

Your emails should address the big picture to determine, for example, how to complete a project as efficiently as possible. Take this approach whether you're starting an email conversation or replying to one of the messages. See how efficiency improves with each version of an email dialogue between Susan and Omar:

Email Dialogue 1: Lots of Wasted Emails

Susan: Please prepare your Q1 expense summary. Let me know if you need expense reports for any prior months and if you can email it to me by April 20. *(Sender clearly states action required)*

Omar: OK, I'll see what I can do. *(Worthless response)*

Omar: I'm working on the summary now and will soon let you know which expense reports I need. *(Another worthless response)*

Omar: I need the January and February expense reports. *(Finally, he explains what he needs.)*

Susan: I'm tied up for the next week. By when do you need these expense reports?

Omar: I need them by April 10, so I can finish the summary by April 20.

Email Dialogue 2: A Bit Better

Susan: Please prepare your Q1 expense summary. Let me know if you need expense reports for any prior months and if you can email it to me by April 20.

Omar: I need the January and February expense reports.

Susan: I'm tied up for the next week. By when do you need these reports?

Omar: I need them by April 10, so I can finish the summary by April 20.

Email Dialogue 3: Efficient, With Explicit Emails From Both Parties

Susan: Omar, please prepare your Q1 expense summary. Let me know if you need expense reports for any prior months and if you can email it to me by April 20.

Omar: Please email me the expense reports for January and February by April 10, and I'll submit the expense summary by April 20. *(He explains what he needs and by when.)*

See this other example illustrating the importance of being explicit, where Larry is trying to schedule a training for his staff with Fang, the conference manager:

Larry: I need to arrange a leadership training course for midlevel managers in March. Are there any training rooms available?

Fang: Let me know how many managers need to be trained so I can provide a suitable room.

Larry: We're looking to put 15 to 20 people through the course.

Fang: I suggest the Royal Conference Room on the fourth floor, which will easily accommodate 20 people.

Larry: Sounds good. Will that room be available during the weeks of March 12 or 19?

Fang: I have Monday, March 12, and Friday, March 23.

Larry: I'd like to avoid Mondays or Fridays. Is there any availability on Tuesdays, Wednesdays, or Thursdays during those weeks?

Fang: The room will be free on Tuesday, March 13, but only until 2 p.m.

Larry: That'll work, because the course is four hours. We can run it from 9 to 1.

Fang: You're confirmed for the Royal Conference Room on March 13, 8 a.m. to 2 p.m. (You can use the extra time for setup and breakdown.)

STEP **9**

It took 10 emails for Larry to arrange the training with Fang. Let's see what happens when Larry is explicit from the start:

> **Larry:** I need to reserve a room for a leadership training course for midlevel managers in March. Please review the details below and let me know what's available.
> - Leadership training:
>   - 4 hours
>   - 15 to 20 midlevel managers
>   - Tuesday, Wednesday, or Thursday during the week of March 12 or 19.
>
> **Fang:** I can give you the Royal Conference Room on the fourth floor, which can easily accommodate 20 people, on Tuesday, March 13, from 8 a.m. to 2 p.m.
>
> **Larry:** That's perfect! We're confirmed for then.

Spur Action With Explicit Subject Lines

How do you decide which emails to open first—or at all? Naturally, it depends on the sender; you'll probably open emails from your boss, a client, or another important party as soon as possible. Otherwise, the subject line is the most critical factor. If a subject line is vague or confusing, you may disregard that email, at least for the time being. Plus, when reading emails on your mobile device, you're more likely to just scan subject lines without reading the body of the messages—which you may read later or not at all.

So as the sender, make your subject lines precise and engaging to increase the chances that the reader will open your email sooner and take the desired action, which will ultimately enhance your productivity.

Compare these three pairs of subject lines:

> **Vague:** Reps' Latest Rating
> **Explicit:** Reps' Rating Down 12% | Need Training
> *What receiver may think upon reading: "I better start planning a training program for the reps."*
>
> **Vague:** Upcoming Budget Meeting
> **Explicit:** May 6 Budget Meeting | Agenda May 3
> *What receiver may think upon reading: "I need to begin working on the agenda."*

Vague: Launch Date
Explicit: Please Approve June 8 Launch Date
What receiver may think upon reading: "I need to decide whether to approve June 8 as a launch date."

Not only is each of these emails with an explicit subject line more likely to be opened sooner than its more-nebulous version, it should prompt the reader to take action—before they read the text of the message.

Don't Be a Lazy Subject Liner

When emailing someone with whom you haven't corresponded in a while (say several months), you may be tempted to search for the last time this person emailed you and simply reply. That's fine, but don't be too lazy to modify the original subject line, which may be unrelated to the topic of your new email. See what happened when Rich didn't bother to change the subject line:

> **POINTER**
>
> Write explicit subject lines so recipients open your emails quickly.

From Christina to Rich (February 20)
- **Subject line:** Q2 Budget Forecasts
- **Text of email:** Please email me your Q2 budget worksheet by March 1.

Eight months later, Rich needs Christina's input on performance reviews. But he's too lazy to change the subject line.

From Rich to Christina (October 22)
- **Subject line:** Re: Q2 Budget Forecasts
- **Text of email:** I'm working on performance reviews. Please email me your scores for the three clerks on your team by October 29.

When Christina, inundated with emails, quickly scans her inbox and sees Rich's subject line, she thinks to herself, "Why is Rich contacting me about the budget worksheets from more than six months ago?" Then she might move onto other emails, leaving Rich without the information he needs before his deadline. Had Rich been

STEP 9

more diligent and inserted a new subject line, such as *Need Clerks' Reviews by Oct. 29,* he probably would've received Christina's input in time.

To further improve email efficiency, sharpen your overall writing ability. The other skills addressed in this book—including brevity, organization, persuasion, tone, and grammar—can all be applied to emails.

Mind Your Etiquette

While many organizations have their own set of rules for sending and receiving emails—frequently related to compliance—follow these practices, universally accepted as proper etiquette:

Make Sure Each Email Would Meet Everyone's Approval

An email is a permanent and documented message, which can be retrieved at any time. Only send messages that comply with your organization's rules and that you would be comfortable showing to any individual at any level or an outside authority. For example, as a midlevel manager, you should never send this type of email criticizing direct reports and the organization's hiring practice: *The new IT assistants don't know the first thing about technology. Where do they find these losers?* If HR department employees or company leaders were to see this email, it would reflect poorly on you as a manager.

Don't Take Shortcuts With Grammar and Syntax

Working professionals used to print out letters, memos, reports, and other documents, sometimes on company letterhead, and mail them out (occasionally, this is still done). The act of producing a physical document compelled employees to carefully review their text and revise if necessary. But the ease of delivering a message with a few keystrokes has resulted in carelessness with spelling, punctuation, capitalization, and sentence structure, not to mention sheer laziness in not using actual words.

STEP 9

POINTER

When writing emails, don't cheat on grammar and don't use funky fonts or text-messaging abbreviations.

Some write emails like a text message (more on texting later). So instead of sending a polished request, *See the operations report for January and email me your comments,* they shoot off emails that read, *c op rpt 4 jan coments bak 2 me.* Once the reader deciphers what the text-speak means (a waste of time and drain on productivity), they will likely consider you less professional.

Avoid Blank Subject Lines

Give your readers a break and clue them in on what the message is about. With the hundreds of emails business workers receive every day, people tend to treat subject lines like headlines in a newspaper or online news outlet: They scan the subject lines and decide which email to open first (as discussed already). A blank subject line can give others the impression that you assume they will open their emails by default, despite not knowing what to expect.

Don't Put the Entire Message in the Subject Line

We've all worked with this co-worker before: You boot up your email in the morning and run into *Can you please review the budget analysis and provide me feedback on the key sections by Feb. 10.* Such a long subject line, while not as bad as no subject line, is difficult to read on mobile devices (see more on making emails mobile-friendly later in this step). A better way to convey this request would be to use a specific subject line, while including the details in the body of the email:

> **Subject:** Budget Analysis Feedback by Feb. 10
> **Text of message:** Please review the budget analysis and provide feedback on the key sections by February 10.

Avoid Putting "Urgent" in the Subject Line

If you want to be known as the panicked employee who needs an immediate response to every issue to avoid a nervous breakdown, then write *urgent* in the subject line. Otherwise, keep *urgent* out of your subject lines. While teaching an undergraduate course several years ago, I had one student who repeatedly wrote *urgent* when sending me emails. Then the message read something like this: "Professor, on the next assignment, should it be three paragraphs or four paragraphs?" In this case, *urgent* was in the eye of the beholder.

Instead, use explicit subject lines and then persuade your reader to action with concise, explicit, and well-organized text. Tool 9-1 offers additional advice to help you keep your email professional.

TOOL 9-1
EMAIL ETIQUETTE QUICK TIPS

For Important Audiences, Use Salutations and Sign-Offs

When emailing senior executives, clients, and other important readers (use your judgment), don't simply begin your message, which can be perceived as too informal. Start with a salutation such as, "Dear Ms. Walker, "Hi Steve," or simply, "Emily." And sign off with something like, "Thanks," "Best regards," or "Best."

Close With a Friendly Outreach

Some argue that ending an email with, "Please contact me if you have any questions," is unnecessary, because the reader knows that they can reply with inquiries. Still, this type of closing sets a positive tone and conveys an important message to the reader—that their opinion matters.

Don't Use All Caps—AND I MEAN IT

An email written in all caps is the written equivalent of shouting. Avoid using email to express anger at someone (See Step 6 on tone).

Avoid Funky Fonts

Not only do artsy and cutesy fonts come across unprofessionally (in most organizations), they can become garbled and unreadable in other email systems.

Stay Away From Colored Backgrounds

Like funky fonts, colored backgrounds can be construed as unprofessional and can make text hard to read.

Save Religious and Spiritual Signatures for Personal Emails

Religious and spiritual messages don't belong on business emails (unless your organization is an institution of this type). Feel free to use an uplifting signature like, "Make it a fulfilling day," but nothing stronger than that.

Lose the Emojis and Emoticons

In many situations, emojis and emoticons can come across as unprofessional. Still, I must admit that some clients and respected colleagues have sent me emails with emojis. Stay away from them unless you're certain that your supervisor or other key people in the company would approve.

Make It Mobile Friendly

Today, more than 60 percent of emails are opened on mobile devices rather than on desktop or laptop computers (Lewkowicz 2016). And this percentage will continue to rise along with the use of mobile devices. Here are the most important tips for ensuring that mobile readers can easily process your emails:

Increase the Font Size

Use at least 12- or 14-point type so the reader doesn't need to squint to read your message. And consider making links even larger.

Limit Subject Lines to 40 to 45 Characters

If you've got too much information to fit within this limit, put the most important message first, as in this example:

Audit Report Revisions May 7 | Senior Partners Must Approve

Be Careful With Bullet Symbols

The different styles of bullet points that Word offers don't always display properly in an email (mobile or otherwise). So stick with simple hyphens or asterisks, as in these two examples:

Among the most profitable products:
- sports drinks
- energy bars
- flavored water.

The keys to marketing success:
* an engaging message
* integrated tactics
* timely follow-up.

Use Single Columns

Text in multiple columns sometimes appears condensed and can be difficult to navigate with certain mobile devices and email systems. Stick with single columns, which will also help you highlight key content.

Be Sure Your Call to Action Stands Out

Make your desired action clearly visible and clickable if you're directing readers to a link. In the following example, the hyperlink to the shipping protocol is bolded:

Please review and approve the **shipping protocol**.

Separate Links With White Space

Avoid closely stacked links, which may cause users to click the wrong one. Compare these two versions (hyperlinks are bolded):

Too Tight–Can Lead to Errors

Learn more about these options for configuring the training room:

- **classroom**
- **u-shaped conference table**
- **clusters.**

Breathing Space–Easier to Click the Right One

Learn more about these options for configuring the training room:

- **classroom**

- **u-shaped conference table**

- **clusters.**

Avoid Large Images

You don't want mobile-device readers frustrated by long delays before your image downloads. Consider shrinking images that may be too large—and then emailing them to yourself so you can test on your mobile device.

Text Like a Professional

Today, business texting (usually through SMS or IM) plays a critical role in helping working professionals communicate faster, internally and externally. About 80 percent of businesspeople text as part of their jobs, according to a 2015 survey conducted by Instantly and commissioned by RingCentral. And nearly 70 percent of employees think their organizations should use texting to communicate internally, according to a 2014 survey by the Vitiello Communications Group.

The first step for enhancing your workplace text messaging is to follow the same guidelines for emails: Keep them brief, get to the point quickly, give clear instructions, check your grammar, and use actual words. Still, texting presents other challenges and opportunities. Here are some tips to for efficient workplace texting:

Avoid Acronyms and Abbreviations

Don't use acronyms or abbreviations (a staple in personal texting) unless you're certain that the receiver knows what you mean. Overusing any type of shorthand could leave your recipient confused and force them to seek out a definition in another app, all to avoid appearing dumb or naive by not knowing it right away.

Divide Long Messages Into Multiple Texts

Instead of cramming too much information and overusing abbreviations to avoid exceeding the character limit, send two or three separate messages. Though that means the individual will receive multiple rings or vibrations, they'll appreciate the more readable messages.

STEP 9

Limit How Much Information You're Asking For

Unlike an email, which can accommodate extensive information (such as with bulleted lists), a text message should be limited to one or two requests. While some people have honed their typing dexterity on mobile devices, you still put a strain on them and less-dexterous users when asking them to type a long reply. Plus, if you ask the reader to research an issue and then report back through text, you're likely asking them to toggle between devices (a computer to research, and a mobile device to reply).

Enable the Reader to Reply Quickly

Structure your text message so the reader can reply immediately with a minimum number of words. An example:

> We will ship your parts by May 8, 10 a.m. CT. Please provide reply with this information:
> - Building number and floor:
> - On-site contact and cell number:
> - Preference—1 large or 3 small containers (indicate 1 or 3):

Know When to Text—and Not to Text

Based on the situation and your organizational culture, determine when text messaging would be the appropriate communication channel as opposed to email or phone. For example, if you need a response within 24 to 48 hours, an email may be the most appropriate medium. But if you're facing a tight deadline and need your supervisor's approval within the hour, a text would probably work best.

Respond to Texts as Soon as Possible

Text messages carry an inherent immediacy about them. Recognize that the sender probably needs your reply within 20 to 30 minutes, just as you do whenever shooting off a text message to a co-worker. You don't want to be known as the one in the office who demands an instant response but doesn't return the favor.

Your Turn

Enhancing the efficiency of your emails and texts requires a variety of strategies to help you save time and compose more effective messages. To hone your email and texting skills, try these exercises:

1. Review this string of messages between two colleagues who have worked together for several years, and determine which of these emails (one or more) aren't necessary:

   > **Rosa:** Please complete the Q4 progress report for XB within two weeks (by January 21) so I can submit it to management for approval.
   > **Marc:** I'll get it to you as soon as I can.
   > **Rosa:** Thanks. I appreciate that.
   > **Marc:** Should it include a summary of prior XB progress reports? And, if so, how far back should I go?
   > **Rosa:** Can you access these prior reports?
   > **Marc:** Yes, I can access XB progress reports from the past two years.
   > **Rosa:** Email the past three XB progress reports covering the first three quarters of last year.

2. Write an explicit subject line for this email to your supervisor—designed to get them to open the email as soon as possible:

   > Our team has developed a plan to significantly increase the number of inquiries while lowering online marketing expenses. By dividing these costs equally among all the divisions, we could send 12 more email blasts in a year and expand our reach with mobile advertising by 25 percent. According to our analysis, by next year, this plan could produce an average of 30 inquiries a month instead of our current average of 15 per month.

3. Reorganize this text message to make it easy for the reader to quickly submit the required information:

   > I need to confirm details for the June 1 presentation skills training. I need to know how many of your direct reports will attend. Which location (River Road or Sax Plaza) is best

for them? And what are their preferred starting times? The trainer can begin at 8, 8:30, or 9.

The Next Step

While the majority of working professionals worldwide regularly write and receive emails, considerably fewer compose social media messages as part of their jobs. But that's changing, as an increasing number of organizations are calling on their employees to generate text for social media channels. So you need to be ready. That's what we'll cover in step 10 (Apply Writing Skills to Social Media Copy).

Step 10

Apply Writing Skills to Social Media Copy

Overview

- Prepare for the surge in on-the-job social media writing.
- Speak one-on-one to readers.
- Craft compelling headlines and chunk your content.
- Extend conversations with your replies.
- Write engaging LinkedIn and Twitter posts.

If you're a small business owner, independent contractor, freelancer, or public relations and marketing professional, you recognize the power of social media to achieve business goals. The rest of you have probably gotten fairly adept at using platforms such as Facebook, Instagram, Pinterest, and Yelp. And you may have posted your profile on LinkedIn, where you interact with workplace peers, friends, and acquaintances.

Over the next several years, get ready for more frequent and intensive workplace "socializing." Many companies have already expanded their use of social media platforms to connect with their staff, customers, potential hires, consultants, and others. That means you'll need to build and continually fine-tune your professional presence on LinkedIn and become more adept at using other social media tools.

Those of you who work for a major corporation may soon participate in (or are already participating in) "employee advocacy," where organizations call upon workers at all levels to help build their brands and deliver key messages to target audiences on Facebook, LinkedIn, Twitter, and other platforms. These initiatives are apparently paying off. A study by Bambu (2017) revealed that companies with employee advocacy programs increased revenues by an average of 26 percent in the first year of implementation.

On top of this trend, an increasing number of organizations are creating their own social enterprise networks to enhance internal communication—beyond the scope of its corporate communication specialists. According to a study by Deloitte, business leaders use social enterprise networks to create a "highly engaged workforce to support them in achieving business goals faster." These networks can enhance a company's capability to share best practices, crowdsource for quicker answers, discover new technology solutions, recognize high-performing employees, and drive cross-functional collaboration.

Whatever the reason, you'll likely be writing more social media copy related to your job or business. And all your Facebook experience crowing about your daughter's gymnastics award or describing the bliss of your tropical vacation may not help you write the results-driven social media text required in the workplace.

To be an effective social media writer, hone the skills addressed in earlier steps, such as simplicity, brevity, flow, organization, persuasion, and tone. Then learn some of the techniques and nuances for writing in various platforms.

Maximizing the impact of social media often requires strategies such as integrating images and videos, timing posts, linking to websites, inserting keywords for search engine optimization, creating hashtags, and more. For our discussion, we'll stick with crafting copy that helps you achieve the desired results. Following are the most important social media writing skills to master, especially for LinkedIn and Facebook. (Plus, the final tips two address specific tips for LinkedIn profiles and Twitter posts).

Stop Readers With Compelling Headlines

If you don't entice readers with an engaging headline, bid them farewell because they won't stick around for the rest. Advertising legend David Ogilvy explains, "On the average, five times as many people read the headline as read the body copy" (Dahl 2007). As with email subject lines (see Step 9), a compelling social media headline (such as for LinkedIn, Facebook, or a blog post) can dramatically increase readership.

Two of the best approaches for headline writing are to be explicit (highlighting the message to follow), or to be intriguing (offering a short tease and compelling readers to stay with it and discover something valuable or fascinating). Here are examples of each type of headline:

Explicit
- To Write Persuasively, Address Readers' Hot Buttons
- Reduce Taxes: Fund an IRA

Intriguing
- Drop Your Cable Plan?
- 5 Tips for Breakthrough Interviews

Speak One-on-One to Readers

Take the conversational style preferred in business writing (see Step 1) to a more personal level. For example, if you're talking with a friend about your frustration contacting a software provider for assistance with your new mobile platform, your dialogue—and social media post—could start like this:

> Do you ever feel like software companies hate talking to real customers?

To embrace this style, imagine yourself in a one-on-one conversation about the topic you're writing about. Don't be afraid to be a bit edgy, as in the previous example. Just keep it civil and professional.

STEP 10

Chunk It

The more we get overloaded with information from traditional and social media channels, the more our attention span shrinks. Most people prefer to process messages in brief sound bites. So keep paragraphs super short and, where appropriate, break up text with subheads (see more in Step 4).

In her blog post offering advice on addressing workplace bullying, Catherine Mattice Zundel (2017), president of Civility Partners, uses a colloquial and captivating lead-in followed by three simple subheads to explain why employees fail to act:

> I've been thinking lately about WHY people don't take action against workplace bullying, and I've come up with three reasons:
>
> **1. Fear.** In the case of workplace bullying, taking action means standing up to the bully. It possibly means standing up to managers who aren't willing to acknowledge it's a problem. What happens if people don't listen? Will the bully retaliate? What problems will taking action create? These questions are answered in the context of fear, so the answers lead people to avoid taking action.
>
> **2. Spotlight.** Many people don't want to be in the spotlight. Why would someone volunteer to be in the spotlight if it meant they will be punished by the bully? Or worse, by the organization?
>
> **3. Apathy.** Some people just don't care enough to take action. Maybe the bullying doesn't bother them personally. Or maybe they think it's normal to be treated that way, so they don't feel compelled to take action against normalcy.

Ask Questions That Prompt Actual Responses

When writing website copy, a newsletter article, or an email blast, you might ask a rhetorical question like, "Are you ready to enjoy higher returns on your IRA?" But on social media sites like LinkedIn,

Facebook, and Twitter, you can engage your audiences by asking questions that seek out responses.

For example, as a realtor looking to build relationships with prospective sellers, you might pose this question: "How satisfied are you with the choice of urgent care centers in your community?" Many readers, especially those who believe these choices are limited, may take advantage of the voice you've given them to air their concerns and opinions. Getting readers to engage is more than half the battle with social media. Once you have their attention, try to convince them to take the desired action, such as signing up for a webcast, attending a conference, or purchasing a product.

Extend the Conversation

Typically, when replying to messages on social media, you want your comment to be meaningful, bettering the chances that the other party will engage with you. Say you're a leadership development consultant and see a tweet from a prominent management consulting firm about a recent trend on managing Millennials. If you respond with a request to set up a meeting to discuss your expertise with Millennial workers, you may be perceived as too aggressive—and there go your chances of starting a relationship. Instead, embellish what was said, perhaps offering a different perspective. Let's play out this scenario on Twitter:

> **ZY Management Consultants tweet**
> Over 50% of Millennials disappointed with communication from supervisors.

> **Your response as leadership consultant**
> @ZYMgmtConsult Millennial workers want more face-to-face communication from bosses, says study.

Through this thoughtful post, you've extended the conversation with the individual at ZY, who will likely view you as a valued source on this topic—and may reply or continue the online dialogue, which could help develop a meaningful relationship.

With LinkedIn Profiles, Immediately Convey Your Value

Anyone who wants to know more about you—recruiters, new business prospects, potential partners, and others—goes to your LinkedIn profile, probably your most important personal branding tool. Even as a small business owner with a dynamic website, you may find that those deciding whether to contact you go first to the LinkedIn profile.

Grab attention with a compelling headline followed by an engaging summary of what you can deliver and your approach—speaking directly to your targeted readers. Use a conventional or off-beat style, depending on factors such as your industry, role, and target audience. For more on writing LinkedIn profiles, see Appendix B.

Write Short, Captivating Tweets

Twitter, the ultimate "sound-bite" channel, permits 140 characters to get your message across, but as with all business communication, if possible, strive to go shorter. With so few words to convey your idea, make each one count with simple, direct messages that spur responses.

Among the strategies for composing effective tweets—depending on the subject—are conveying a clear call to action, creating urgency, evoking an emotional response, and piggybacking on breaking news or trends. Let's look at some examples of engaging tweets:

HubSpot (@HubSpot)
72.6% of salespeople using social media outperformed their colleagues who were not on social media.

Maria Shriver (@mariashriver)
What do you do if you're told you're too aggressive?

YearUp (@YearUp)
Hiring a cookie-cutter team can stifle innovation. Why employers need to look outside the box.

Deloitte (@Deloitte)
Thirsty for a change: The untapped potential of women in urban water management.

Your Turn

To get others to read your social media copy, you need to captivate them instantly with as few words as possible. Try this exercise to hone your skills in grabbing attention:

Imagine that you're either applying for a new job or trying to land a new client. The decision maker has asked all candidates to tweet something compelling about yourself or your company. Compose a tweet that summarizes your most important value-added quality (perhaps from information on your LinkedIn profile) to convince the individual to select you.

Appendix A

Drive Organizational and Personal Success With Better Writing

So you believe poor writing is hurting your organization. The emails and other documents from certain individuals—ranging from senior executives and supervisors to first-line managers and new hires—aren't up to speed. If you want to enhance their writing in a way that produces meaningful improvements and achieves key goals, follow this course of action:

- Recognize the writing–outcomes link.
- Identify who needs to upgrade writing skills.
- Get management buy-in.
- Design the training course.
- Cultivate a writing culture.
- Develop a writing style guide.

If you're not responsible for others' performance and want to hone your own skills, see "Improve Your Writing" at the end of this appendix.

Recognize the Writing-Outcomes Link

"Good writing is so important. I'd love to get our staff to write better." For years, I've heard these types of comments from learning and development or human resource professionals, senior executives, and business owners. Though many are quick to disparage their employees' writing, far fewer people in these roles understand how writing affects organizational success—and those who do often have difficulty explaining it to management. Plus, the leaders who control the purse strings are often unwilling to make a significant investment in an apparently "intangible" initiative.

If you want to upgrade employees' writing abilities, start by identifying your organization's key measures of success, such as productivity, profitability, and engagement. Then try to link effective writing to each measure, and determine the negative consequences of poor or mediocre writing. These could include wasted time rereading convoluted emails, clients annoyed by offensive messages, leaders unable to motivate employees, and many more.

One of the best places to find out more about writing issues is from employees throughout the organization who recognize shortcomings in co-workers' text and understand how they hurt. Those critics may include C-suite executives, division heads, line managers, or others. Complaints may even come from rank-and-file workers whose productivity is being stifled by cryptic messages from other departments or who resent the steady stream of rude emails from supervisors. You might also discover that clients are annoyed by your employees' emails, which could be unclear, condescending, or riddled with grammar errors and typos.

Identify Who Needs to Upgrade Writing Skills

Sometimes poor writing starts at the top. A surprising number of high achievers have risen through the ranks with substandard writing ability, partly because the business community traditionally didn't value good writing. Their prowess in managing others, generating leads, and closing deals has catapulted them to the top of the organizational chart. But at some point, most of these individuals assume a new leadership role that requires them to write more. While a select few can call upon the corporate communications team to compose their messages, most leaders who write their own text often fall short in many ways. These include confusing directives, an offensive rather than a supportive tone, the inability to persuade others to embrace their ideas, and the failure to engage the staff. As a result, the organization suffers.

To proactively identify individuals who need to improve their writing, consider these tactics:

- Contact those with responsibility for staff performance—including HR or learning directors, division heads, managers, and other key players—and ask them to assess the writing abilities of their direct reports and other employees with whom they interact. Also request sample emails or documents (with proprietary information deleted). If you receive too many writing examples for you to read on your own, build a team of people to review them. Then, based on the assessments and the samples, determine which individuals or groups would benefit most from writing instruction.
- Discreetly ask senior leaders if they believe elevating their writing proficiency would help them achieve better results.
- Solicit feedback from clients, suppliers, and others outside the organization with whom your employees correspond. Ask them to rate such measures as clarity, brevity, organization, and tone.

While many employees designated for a writing training will jump at the chance to upgrade their skills, others may feel offended that they were singled out for an apparent "writing deficiency." Be sure to position these learning programs not as remedial but as a valuable opportunity to hone writing abilities, enhance productivity, and even help secure a promotion. Point out that even the most proficient business writers can learn new techniques that lead to better results for themselves and for the organization.

Get Management Buy-In

Before making the case to decision makers and securing resources for a writing course, reflect on your organizational culture: How much does your company value written communication and recognize its power to fuel better outcomes? (See the section on building a culture that values writing.) Your assessment may affect your strategy for presenting the program to management, including the breadth of the proposed training course and the method of evaluation.

Even executives who appreciate the difference better writing can make may be leery of allocating dollars to improve skills that they don't believe can be directly tied to achieving profitability or preventing disasters. They tend to favor initiatives that can produce tangible benefits, such as training in sales, software, and cybersecurity. For these decision makers, point out that enhanced writing abilities drive results in productivity, employee engagement, new business development, and other areas. Bolster your case with findings from studies linking poor writing to poor outcomes (see "The Demand for Good Writing" in the introduction).

To better your chances for management approval, explain that you'll develop reliable methods to track the effectiveness of the training course, including follow-up surveys with participants and their supervisors and before-and-after evaluations of participants' writing. You can also assess other measures of success, such as more-engaged employees (for leaders) and higher productivity, before and after the training course.

Design the Training Course

Even if you don't work for a learning organization with a ton of resources, you can still design an effective learning program that produces measurable outcomes. Here are some key steps:

Establish Preliminary Goals

Clarify the desired outcomes, such as enhancing email productivity, building relationships with clients through thoughtful and professional messages, or creating a more robust social media presence through compelling text.

Choose the Instructor

Should you choose an in-house or outside instructor? First look at the expertise within your learning or HR department, especially experienced facilitators who may be familiar with the targeted employees' strengths and weaknesses. If one of the in-house trainers has experience teaching writing, they could be an ideal choice.

Another resource is the corporate communications or public relations department, staffed by those whose job it is to write for the company. But keep in mind that being able to *do* and being able to *teach* are separate skills. Your ideal instructor should be able to do both. Also realize that you're asking a person to take on an extra task on top of their regular workload. Will they be willing to put time into designing a learning program for employees in another department? It may take a senior leader to make it happen.

If in-house trainers aren't available or if you don't believe they bring enough expertise to teach business writing, then hire an outside instructor. Find them the same way you find other facilitators—through referrals, online searches, and the local chapter of ATD.

Ask the instructor candidates to submit information about themselves, along with references and links to their websites, LinkedIn profiles, and other forms of online presence. Plus, watch a sample presentation video, if they have one. Be sure to speak to the instructor candidates, either in person or over the phone, before signing a contract. An email won't reveal a person's commitment to success or willingness to tailor the course to the participants' needs. Listen to how they come across and let your instincts tell you if they're a good fit for your organization.

Develop Objectives

Work with the instructor to set specific objectives, building on your preliminary goals. For example, if you want a certain group of employees to improve their email efficiency, one program objective would be to compose explicit emails that reduce the number of back-and-forth messages. Then you could compare the average number of emails to complete a task before and after the training to evaluate its success.

Tailor the Program to Participants' Requirements

Collaborate with the instructor to develop a training course that pinpoints the employees' needs. Start with a needs analysis that includes a review of participants' writing samples and separate surveys for participants and their supervisors. Among the information to uncover about the learners:

- toughest writing challenges
- percentage of day spent writing
- attitude toward writing—enjoy, tolerate, or dislike
- frequently written emails and documents
- perceived proficiency in competencies such as grammar, brevity, flow, organization, tone, persuasion, and email efficiency
- expected outcomes from improved writing.

Work with the instructor to analyze the samples and survey results so you can design a program best suited to the participants' needs.

Select Learning Delivery Methods

Today you can choose myriad learning options—including classroom, webinars, one-on-one coaching, online self-study, and mobile tutorials. Decide what method or combination of methods is most practical based on factors such as office locations, learner preference, and resources. If your budget is limited, consider enrolling employees in a writing course at a local college or registering them in online training. Be sure to preview the self-study courses and ensure they've been designed by a reputable business writing expert.

One-on-One Coaching

The ability to work privately with a coach—in a comfortable, nonthreatening environment—allows people at all levels to address their toughest writing challenges and often dramatically improve the quality of their typical emails and documents. These sessions are particularly valuable to "writing introverts" less likely to ask to talk about their writing in a group setting. In my writing workshops, usually with 15 to 20 people, only about a third of the learners frequently raise their hands, point out corrections to the intentional mistakes on the screen, or read their revised versions of exercises aloud.

One-on-one writing coaching sessions can also be incorporated as a follow-up to a group workshop. Each participant could receive a designated number of 45- to 60-minute sessions, in person or over the phone, enabling them to practice skills learned in the workshop and to apply them to on-the-job emails and documents.

When a workshop is not offered, consider a dedicated coaching program of eight to 12 sessions for targeted employees. These private sessions, designed to achieve key objectives, could prove especially valuable to those struggling with their writing (including international professionals). Plus, managers at different levels could enhance their leadership prowess by learning to craft messages that demonstrate their ability to understand a problem or situation and recommend logical, easy-to-follow next steps. After the final coaching session, the instructor should develop a brief analysis that explains progress made, areas for improvement, and suggestions for ongoing self-study.

Executive Writing Coaching

As face-to-face meetings and phone calls give way to emails, texts, and other computer-mediated communication, C-suite executives are writing more messages than ever—to colleagues, direct reports, rank-and-file employees, clients, and others. This written communication often deals with critical and sensitive topics like shifts in corporate strategy, complex organizational changes, and internal strife.

Through dedicated one-on-one coaching, those in the C-suite can learn to compose these important messages in a way that demonstrates their leadership capabilities. These private, discreet programs could focus on skills such as engaging employees by tapping their hot buttons, using a productive tone when pointing out shortcomings, and conveying the company's value to clients and prospects.

Build Sustainability Tools

To maximize benefits from a writing training program, offer options that enable participants to continue honing their skills after the workshops, webinars, and coaching sessions have concluded. Consider integrating microlearning tools like mobile tutorials that employees could easily access as needed. For example, a first-line manager who receives a harsh or condescending email could instantly access a two-minute video explaining how to compose a civil and appropriate reply. See if the instructor can provide tutorials that complement the learning delivered thus far.

Cultivate a Writing Culture

When a company and its leaders show that they understand how effective writing can drive success throughout the enterprise, this message will filter down to managers and personnel at all levels. As a result, employees will recognize their responsibility to upgrade their writing skills and appreciate the support from those at the top.

Strategies for demonstrating that the organization values high-quality writing include:

- Make writing one of the competencies assessed in performance reviews.
- Publish expectations about the quality of writing in the employee handbook, including the types of email and documents that should be mastered by those in certain positions.
- Promote a collaborative writing atmosphere where co-workers review and critique each other's drafts, and establish writing support groups.
- Encourage employees to submit content to internal newsletters, social enterprise networks, and other internal communication channels—and reward authors of the best-written pieces with gifts, vacation time, or other incentives.

Onboard With Writing Training

The best time to improve employees' writing and truly foster a writing culture is when they're first hired. By embedding writing training into a new employee onboarding program, the organization will help ensure that those in new positions enhance their writing proficiency, master frequently written emails and documents, and adhere to the company's structure and format. Plus, these new hires will learn how to shape their writing to model the behavior and style the company expects.

Work with your internal or external instructor to design a writing program that would fit seamlessly into your existing onboarding process. The training could start with, for instance, a three-hour live workshop or webinar on core business writing skills, followed by self-study modules, one-on-one coaching, mobile tutorials, or other methods.

Develop a Writing Style Guide

One way to make employees immediately more comfortable with their writing is to create a style guide with guidelines for capitalization, expressing numbers, abbreviations, fonts, layout, and more.

Here are some rules your corporate style guide could include:

- For numbers, spell out zero to nine, and use numerals for 10 and above.
- Express numbers in the millions or higher in a decimal format ($7.5 million instead of $7,500,000). Naturally, financial reports with tables in which exact amounts are presented would be an exception to this rule.
- For names, use both the given name and the surname on first reference; use the last name for all subsequent references. And avoid courtesy titles like *Mr., Miss, Ms.,* or *Mrs.*
- Write time in numeral format: 10 a.m., 7:30 p.m.
- Use two-letter standard postal abbreviations for states (NY, CA, OH, and so forth).

- To avoid reader confusion with acronyms, spell out the name or phrase the first time it's used and enclose the acronym in parentheses immediately after it. Here's an example: *Our industry needs to better understand the potential impact of artificial intelligence (AI)*.
- Don't use all-caps type for the regular text portion of any document because it's more difficult to read.
- Don't capitalize generic titles such as *division head* or *regional manager*.
- Use standard round bullets.

That list is far from exhaustive. Draft a guide that answers the needs of your employees and is pertinent to your most frequently written emails and documents. The guide shouldn't drive employees crazy with seemingly insignificant rules; instead, it should help workers stop wasting time trying to decide whether to write *Ms. Hunter* or *Hunter* when drafting a meeting summary.

Treat the style guide as a living document, which should be updated periodically as new questions arise or new types of emails or documents become part of the corporate mix. One person or a team in the learning or HR department could be assigned the task of establishing the new rules and continually updating the guide.

Also as part of the style guide, you can include document templates and boilerplate language for certain categories of emails and text messages. A template establishes the look of a document—the typefaces used for text and headlines, the margins, the layout for charts or tables, and so forth. Boilerplate language is standard wording that employees can access and update with data pertinent to the communication at hand. For example, an employee first would download the boilerplate language for an email to a customer acknowledging receipt of a complaint and the company's next steps. Then they would plug in the complaint details, the recommended solution, and other pertinent information before sending the message.

Improve Your Writing

If you're not part of the learning and development or human resource team and don't oversee other workers (or even if you do), you may want to improve your own writing skills. Start by envisioning what benefits would come your way as a stronger writer. These could range from a dynamic LinkedIn profile that helps you land a better job, compelling new business proposals that generate leads, and robust social media posts that spark dialogue with key contacts. Or you may just want the personal satisfaction that comes from being a more proficient writer. The more clearly you can identify the potential payoff of better writing, the easier it will be to motivate yourself to do what it takes to achieve your objectives.

Then identify the skills (see the steps in this book) most important for you to master. You may just want a general refresher in several areas, to write faster with more confidence, or to persuade prospects to purchase your services. By pinpointing desired improvements, you'll be able to develop a plan to attain your goals. Here are some options:

- Go solo—teach yourself to write better by going through each step in this book, completing the exercises and continuing to practice.
- Find out if your organization plans to offer a business writing course in the next 12 months, and, if so, register.
- Retain a writing coach who will review your challenges and goals and design a coaching program tailored to your requirements.
- Enroll in a live writing course or webinar taught by a reputable writing instructor.
- Complete a self-study business writing course from a well-respected provider.
- Watch brief writing videos on topics related to your specific needs to help you sustain your skills.

Appendix B

Master the Text You Write Most Often

The writing skills addressed in this book can be applied to virtually all types of emails, text messages, and documents used in the business world. Still, you should develop techniques to improve the quality of what you write most often. In this appendix, you'll find strategies for writing the following documents, along with examples:

- performance review
- audit report
- proposal
- email to irritated customer
- presentation slides
- project status report
- press release
- LinkedIn profile summary.

Performance Review

If you were asked by a senior executive to summarize your direct report's performance out loud in 30 seconds, your reply might go something like this:

> Chung Lee is a hard-working relationship manager whose customer satisfaction ratings topped all his colleagues, but he had an 11 percent error rate on orders (more than the expected 5 percent) and needs to become a better team player.

When writing a performance review, consider starting with that type of big-picture approach: Summarize the person's strengths, challenges, overall performance during the past six to 12 months, and your recommendations. For more negative reviews, however, you may not want to put too much bad news up front.

Many companies require performance evaluators to follow a template and answer specific questions, which can make it difficult to describe certain aspects of the employee's accomplishments or development opportunities. In those cases, see if you can add an introductory paragraph to sum up the individual's performance.

See Tool B-1 for two suggested outline options you can use to write performance reviews, which can be modified to fit your company's template. The sample performance review (Example B-1) uses the second outline option.

Tool B-1
Two Outlines for Performance Reviews

Option 1

Overview: Big picture in two or three sentences
Strengths (Goals met or exceeded):
- Product knowledge
- Customer support interactions
- Working with team
Challenges (Goals not met):
- Product knowledge

- Customer support interactions
- Working with team

Recommendations: Performance improvement plan, training, promotion, and so forth

Option 2

Overview: Big picture in two or three sentences
Product knowledge:
- Strengths
- Challenges

Phone skills:
- Strengths
- Challenges

Working with team:
- Strengths
- Challenges

Recommendations: Performance improvement plan, training, promotion, and so forth

EXAMPLE B-1

SAMPLE PERFORMANCE REVIEW USING OPTION TWO

Employee: Carmella Rojas, account representative
Performance period: October 15, 2016, to October 15, 2017

Overview

A hard-working account representative, Carmella Rojas consistently handles more phone calls than required and scores high on customer service. Carmella has demonstrated an ability to grasp personal lines products, but has difficulty understanding commercial lines products. To be promoted to the next level, she needs to improve her commercial lines knowledge and spend more time helping colleagues to show that she's a team player.

The first paragraph sums up the employee's performance over the past 12 months.

Product Knowledge
Strengths
With two years' experience in auto, home, and flood insurance, Carmella has an intimate knowledge of

Each of the three
performance cate-
gories is divided
into *Strengths* and
Challenges.

all personal lines products, and has learned the new provisions as they've been introduced.

Challenges

Carmella has struggled to understand commercial lines because she lacks experience with these policies. The few customer complaints against her have concerned commercial lines. She needs to spend more time learning these products.

Phone Skills

Strengths

Over the past 12 months, Carmella has handled an average of 15 percent more calls than required for this position. Plus, her customer service rating has been 8 of 10 or higher for the entire period. In that time, only two official customer complaints have been filed against her, the lowest number received for any member of the team.

Challenges

The only area in which Carmella needs to improve is explaining commercial lines products. She often speaks too quickly to customers—perhaps to hide her uncertainty—and some people have called or emailed to request clarification.

Working With a Team

Strengths

Many less-experienced account representatives have a better grasp of personal lines policies thanks to Carmella's coaching and willingness to answer their questions.

Challenges

Carmella tends to help others on her team only when asked. She should be reaching out to other account representatives more often, letting them know she's available to help. Given her extensive product knowledge, she could be a far greater asset to the rest of the team.

Recommendations

Carmella Rojas, who has proven to be an asset to the team, could be ready for a promotion within the next six months. Over the next three months, she should complete the team dynamics course, which can teach her the keys to working better with team members. Plus, she should attend the weekly sales meeting whenever a commercial lines product is addressed. If Carmella demonstrates significant improvement as a team player and in commercial lines after completing these steps, she should be promoted to account manager.

This section provides Carmella with specific next steps and how she could be promoted.

Audit Report

Audit reports are prepared in many different fields, including accounting, pharmaceuticals, and manufacturing. An effective audit report should first state the purpose of the audit and the most pertinent conclusion to immediately convey the general outcome. Then the report should explain all facets of the audit in a logical sequence, including details of the process.

It also may include lists, such as people interviewed, key observations, and the supporting documents attached. The product-specific audit for a contract supplier presented in Example B-2 suggests sections that might be applicable to audits in your organization. See how the specific topics are separated into clearly organized paragraphs and defined with descriptive subheads.

EXAMPLE B-2
EXTERNAL AUDIT FOR XY COMPANY'S QUALIFICATIONS AS PACKAGING OPERATION FOR PRODUCT Z

Purpose

With the purpose and conclusion up front, the reader immediately grasps the big picture.

This audit was conducted to assess the capability of XY Company to perform labeling, secondary packaging, and distribution of Product Z, especially regarding the control of supplies from start to finish.

Conclusion

XY Company is qualified to perform labeling, secondary packaging, and distribution of Product Z.

General Methods

A three-person team conducted the audit through conference room discussions, interviews with employees, and reviews of selected documentation in relevant areas.

Location

The audit was conducted at the XY Company's Portland, Maine, facility, a 110,000-square-foot building devoted to primary and secondary blister packaging.

Summary of Findings

- The packaging areas were neat, clean, and well organized, which promoted a smooth, well-run operation.
- The receiving area was congested because of the high volume of material received.

The quick snapshot of the two findings prepares the reader for the following details.

Specific Findings

1. Receipt and storage areas: Materials received are hand-recorded on receiving documents, transferred to a computerized quality inventory system, and inspected. XY Company is constructing a self-contained sampling booth for raw materials. Once checked, the materials are moved to a staging corridor and held until ready for processing. The corridor was well organized, except for a few partially broken pallets not properly aligned in the racks.

Observation A: One end of each storage rack is identified by a number (for example, C203) and the other end is identified with the same number. The pallet spaces between are designated C203A, C203B, C203C, and so forth, but are not labeled as such. That could result in an improper pallet being pulled from the racks.

Observation B: Package inserts are commingled in the storage area with general packaging materials, a procedure not recognized as an industry standard.

2. Manufacturing, in-process storage, and warehouse areas: The manufacturing areas were neat and clean, efficient, and optimized for work flow. The movement of materials was well orchestrated and performed in a manner that suggested it was well controlled. The primary packaging areas were self-contained and meticulously clean. Because of space constraints, finished products were staged in the warehouse area and then moved to the off-site warehouse, where they awaited final disposition.

The four recommendations are presented with bullet points rather than with numerals because they don't need to be completed in a particular sequence.

Recommendations

- Maintain a person in the plant during all packaging operations.
- Review and sign master packaging record.
- Review and accept each batch production record.
- Review and accept all deviations that may occur during packaging.

Proposal

To get prospects to hire your firm, to get supervisors or colleagues to approve your plan, or to get others to say yes to any initiative, you need to hook them right away. Begin proposals with a concise, convincing argument on why the readers should embrace your ideas—focusing them on your mode of reasoning and enticing them to review the entire document. With new business proposals, the opening should reflect the prospect's needs (rather than your skills) and offer ways your company can satisfy these needs.

The rest of the proposal should elaborate on what you've addressed in the opening, presented in a logical sequence. You should also write a compelling title, a task that's often easier to do after you've drafted some or all of the document.

For a new business proposal, sections could include objectives, target audiences, strategies, and tactics (see Example B-3). Note that other parts of a typical proposal (such as budget, timeline, and the firm's qualifications) haven't been included.

EXAMPLE B-3
NEW BUSINESS PROPOSAL

Powerful, Consistent Messages to Build the Indiana Association of Working Professionals (IAWP) Brand

The title conveys the key concept: powerful, consistent messages.

Overview: Consistent Messages to Build Visibility

To help IAWP build its brand, increase membership, and drive its legislative agenda, GXX Partners can develop compelling messages that highlight the critical value it offers members. GXX, with a track record in helping associations achieve their communication goals, can craft a series of powerful messages targeted to members, prospects, legislators, and other key audiences.

The opening introduces the primary idea—compelling messages that highlight the association's value—and states why GXX can produce the desired results.

These messages will include how IAWP's educational programs enhance management abilities, how supporting IAWP's legislative initiatives can improve a company's bottom line, and how networking at IAWP can generate new business leads.

Goals
- Build IAWP's brand as the voice of the industry.
- Help recruit more members.
- Demonstrate the value of IAWP membership, such as educational programs, a voice with the state legislature, updates on industry trends, and discounts on various services.
- Support IAWP's legislative agenda.

Target Audiences
- Current and prospective IAWP members
- Key legislators
- Other key Indiana business leaders and organizations
- Key Indiana media

Strategy: Reshape Messages to Address "What's in It for Me?"

The strategy explains the key idea: reshaping IAWP's messages.

The key to achieving the objectives is composing clear and powerful messages that convey the value that IAWP offers. GXX will guide IAWP in reshaping messages so they speak directly to the audience's needs. Although IAWP has been promoting member benefits for many years, its messages to explain them need to better answer the question, "What's in it for me?"

Among the potential messages:
- IAWP's programs help you improve management skills and grow your business.
- IAWP's member benefits, including shipping discounts, offer bottom-line savings.
- IAWP's job retraining programs serve an essential role in the business community.

Tactics: Deliver Consistent Messages Through Many Vehicles

To deliver its messages effectively, IAWP should incorporate several tactics. These could include e-newsletters, monthly email blasts, an expanded social media presence, and mobile ads. These vehicles would work together to deliver the association's messages consistently.

This section describes the means for implementing the strategy.

Email to Irritated Customer

Even if all aspects of your company run perfectly, customers will get upset from time to time. Maybe the product they bought is defective, they've been charged an amount they don't think is justified, your customer service reps haven't returned their emails, or there was a delay in promised service. It doesn't matter if these issues are real or perceived; the customer must be reassured and satisfied.

The language you use in replying to a customer or business client will go a long way in building loyalty and determining how your organization is perceived in the marketplace. (See Step 6 for more about setting the right tone.) This is especially critical today when negative reviews on the growing number of online consumer forums can quickly damage your reputation—and your bottom line. Tool B-2 offers suggestions on correspondence with customers who are annoyed with the company. And see Example B-4 for these tips in action.

Tool B-2
Tips for Writing to Unhappy Customers

- Address the customer's specific complaint instead of offering a canned response that comes across as phony and insincere.
- If your firm has made a mistake, admit it without making excuses, and empathize with the inconvenience that was caused.
- Don't patronize the customer with trite language such as, "At XZ Company, we love all our loyal customers."
- If the customer is wrong, don't insult their intelligence or motives. Point out how the individual could have thought they were right and the company was wrong, and carefully lay out the facts of the disputed matter.
- Research what you can offer and explain it in your reply. This could include a gift card, a discount coupon, or free delivery on upcoming orders.

- Provide the customer with a quick and painless way to contact you, such as a direct email, a direct phone line, or a cell number to text you.

EXAMPLE B-4
EMAIL TO IRRITATED CUSTOMER

Dear Ms. Santana,

We apologize that your refrigerator was delivered six hours late—no customer should be inconvenienced to that degree. To help make up for our mistake, we've enclosed a $50 gift card that can be used anywhere.

We also understand your disappointment in being charged a $75 delivery fee when you expected it to be free. While you're correct that this offer was good on orders processed through June 30 (and yours was placed June 22), the free delivery was limited to homes within a 20-mile radius of our location. Your house is 32 miles from our store. We understand how easily you could've misunderstood the terms of our offer—as did several other customers. So we'll be sure to clarify our upcoming promotions. Plus, we've enclosed a 20 percent off coupon for any item in our store, valid for 12 months.

Thanks for being our customer, and we hope you'll continue purchasing our products and give us the opportunity to improve our service to you in the future. Please feel free to call me on my direct line (888.555.6349).

Sincerely,

Latisha Freemont, Senior Account Manager

The opening empathizes with Ms. Santana without patronizing her and immediately offers a makeup gift.

This paragraph again empathizes with her about the unexpected delivery fee and explains the terms of the offer without insulting her intelligence—underscored by the fact that other customers have made the same mistake.

The closing makes a genuine appeal to the customer to continue shopping at the store and offers an easy method of contact.

Presentation Slides

You may have heard the expression "death by PowerPoint," referring to agonizingly boring presentations by speakers who clog the screen with too much text and put their audiences to sleep. But PowerPoint (and similar presentation programs) is a valuable communication tool that's gotten a bad rap thanks to its widespread misuse.

While tools such as graphs, music, videos, and animated visuals can enhance the effectiveness of a presentation, the following tips focus primarily on composing the text while including some basic layout guidelines. Use them as your speaking outline to keep yourself on track and to keep your audience centered on what you're saying. Don't write every word you plan to say on the slide; otherwise, your audience will tune you out and read ahead on the slides.

Compare the following three pairs of slides that comprise a portion of a marketing proposal.

Example 1

Wordy	Concise
Marketing Objectives: • We need to achieve a 15 percent higher market share. • We should be able to generate 500 more leads by targeting the energy sector. • We can expand our reach in the Southeast region.	Marketing Objectives: • 15 percent more market share • 500 more leads in energy sector • Expanded reach in Southeast

Example 2

Wordy	Concise
Tactics: • Write and distribute email blasts to our database of clients and prospects in the Southeast region. • Implement SEO targeted to key cities in the Southeast. • Develop banner ads to post on key websites read by those in the energy sector.	Tactics: • Email blasts: clients and prospects in Southeast • SEO: key Southeast cities • Banner ads: energy sector sites

Example 3

Wordy	Concise
Next Steps: • Conduct a brainstorming session to help develop key concepts to deliver our messages. • Instruct creative team to produce banner ad campaigns to present to us for evaluation. • Develop copy for the email blasts and the SEO campaign for our review.	Next Steps: • Brainstorm banner ad concepts. • Create banner ad campaigns. • Write email and SEO copy.

See Tool B-3 for best practices in developing slides.

Tool B-3
Tips for Creating Effective Slides

Slides should be the ideal complement to your presentation if they're created with an appealing combination of text and layout.

Text

- Use short phrases and sentences instead of long sentences.
- Use a consistent, parallel structure within each slide, such as by making each line a command or a question.
- To save space:
  - Omit short words like *the, in,* and *of* whenever possible.
  - Abbreviate; for example "Feb." for "February" and "TBD" for "to be decided."
  - Replace "and" with an ampersand (&).
  - Replace words with colons, dashes, or slashes; for example, instead of "Mobile marketing for new health app," write "Mobile marketing: new health app."

Layout

- Don't clutter a slide with too much text; write no more than six lines.
- For headlines, use 36-point type or larger; for text, use 24-point type or larger.
- Stick to one or two typefaces.
- Minimize the amount of text you put in all caps because it's more difficult to read.
- Frequently use bullets or numerals to group items.
- Choose combinations of background and text color that are easiest to read.
- Test the readability of your slides by projecting them on a screen and moving far enough away to simulate viewing from the back of the room where you'll be presenting.

Project Status Report

While the content and format of status reports can vary significantly, virtually all are designed to provide a quick snapshot of an upcoming or ongoing project. The report should help your management team make better decisions about the direction of the project. It may be submitted as a word processing or spreadsheet document (sometimes in a template) or within the text of an email.

Your report needs to demonstrate that you understand all aspects of the project through a concise, well-organized document, which, if necessary, should include recommended solutions to key problems. Still, there should be no surprises, because this is not the place to share bad news for the first time.

Here are guidelines for an effective status report, which can be applied to many different types of projects. These suggestions came with the assistance of Elizabeth Harrin, a project management specialist and director of Otobos Consultants.

Start With the Big Picture

If readers aren't aware of the project's context, explain the project in a nutshell. This two- or three-sentence description could include the scope, objectives, challenges, and other key information. Call it an executive summary, project overview, or other appropriate name. If your report goes to people who know the project well and who want a progress update, begin with a summary of major points from that reporting period before going into detail.

Consider Your Audience

What do your readers want to know about the project? For example, with projects on a tight budget, your manager might want an update on how much has been spent thus far and anticipated expenditures. If it's critical that you hit a certain launch date, explain whether you're still on track to meet the deadline. Don't be afraid to tailor your report for the people receiving it.

Discuss Results Rather Than Activities

Nobody wants to plow through every last detail of what you did. Focus on major achievements and the business implications. Mention if you're deviating from your original plans, such as delivering something early or shifting tasks around, and explain how upcoming milestones or deadlines will change.

Highlight Action Items

Call attention to decisions you're awaiting from management. Explain what you're doing to manage risks and issues on the project.

Divide the Report Into Logical Sections

Depending on the subject matter and your company's format, create sections that flow logically from start to finish. Here's one way to outline a project status report:

1. Executive summary
2. Work completed
3. Work in progress
4. Work to be completed
5. Issues and recommended solutions
6. Actions and decisions required

See Example B-5 for a typical project status report.

EXAMPLE B-5
PROJECT STATUS REPORT ON CONSTRUCTION OF NEW WAREHOUSE

The opening gives a quick overview about the project, including start and completion dates and the major obstacle thus far.

Project Status Report: Construction of Sutton Street Warehouse

Date: January 16

Executive Summary

The construction of a 96′ x 144′ warehouse on Sutton Street to store raw materials (approved October 9 with expected completion June 4) is on schedule and proceeding smoothly. The biggest challenge is an unanticipated rise in the cost of materials from the plumbing contractor, for which we've reached a temporary agreement so work won't be delayed. We're currently negotiating a long-term solution.

Work Completed
- Plans approved by the county Department of Development and Permits (Nov. 12)
- Lines laid out by plumbing and electrical contractors (Dec. 2)
- Foundation poured (Dec. 10)

Work in Progress (With Expected Completion Dates)
- Installation of high-level lighting, socket outlets, and alarm systems (Jan. 24)
- Construction of building exterior, including metal roofing and prefinished walls (Feb. 7)
- Installation of sprinkler system (March 2)

Work to Be Completed (With Targeted Completion Dates)
- Install sanitary piping, plumbing fixtures, and energy-efficient HVAC unit (March 29).
- Install epoxy floor system (April 3).
- Paint the interior (April 10).
- Install storage rack system (April 26).
- Secure certificate of occupancy from county building inspector (May 6).

Issues and Recommended Solutions
Issue 1: XCX Plumbing increased materials costs 15 percent, effective January 1, after procurement had apparently signed an agreement October 11 with last year's pricing. But a closer review of the contract language revealed that pricing terms were unclear.

Recommendation: Accept the price increase if XCX agrees to provide six months of service (instead of the typical three months) at no charge. Given our anticipated spending for service in that period, we should, at worst, break even.

Issue 2: ZD Floor Coatings notified us that the delivery of the epoxy floors in our preferred color scheme wouldn't arrive until April 15, too late to keep this project on track.

Recommendation: Instruct ZD to order a comparable color scheme that we've already approved and which ZD guaranteed would arrive by March 28.

Actions and Decisions Required

- Approve our recommended agreement negotiated with XCX Plumbing.
- Confirm that we can order the epoxy floor in the new color scheme from ZD Floor Coatings.
- Select either multitier racking or pallet racking (see links to photos, specifications, and price comparisons).
- Choose a two-color paint scheme for the interior walls (see link to five potential combinations).

Press Release

Despite the social media revolution that continues to transform the practice of public relations, the press release remains one of the most important vehicles for delivering messages. And, with the proliferation of sites such as LinkedIn, Facebook, Twitter, and others, most press releases reach a larger audience of not only media members but also consumers and other end users. So if you're a PR practitioner or play a role in promoting your company, you should know how to craft effective press releases that support your organization's communication.

Your toughest challenge with any press release is getting past gatekeepers—newspaper editors, TV producers, bloggers, and so forth. These individuals, often swamped with more than 100 releases a day, select only a small percentage of them to use in some way, such as to generate a major story, to include a portion in a publication or website, or mention on the air. The rest of the press releases are rejected for a variety of reasons: irrelevant to their audience, lack of news value, too much hype, bland text, poorly written, and more. The winners that rise to the top in are the concise, organized, and well-written releases that convey their major news in the headline and lead, and that flesh out the story in brief paragraphs arranged in a logical sequence.

Before you get past the gatekeepers, you need to stop them with a captivating headline (often in the subject line) and a compelling lead. As one editor told me, "If the copy doesn't excite me in the first 20 words, I won't read the rest of it."

One way to write gripping headlines and leads is to look beyond the obvious facts about your product, service, event, or issue to uncover its most significant news value. Let's look at some techniques for creating newsworthy headlines and leads.

Captivating Headlines

Visualize how the story you want to tell would come across in one of your targeted newspapers, magazines, TV broadcasts, blogs, or other channels. Then craft a headline that grabs their attention and intrigues the individual enough to continue reading.

Compare these two headlines and see how the second one conveys legitimate news (75 new hires):

> **Headline 1:** ZY's Q3 Profits Increase 10%, CEO Cites "New Opportunities" for Growth
>
> **Headline 2:** ZY Profit Up 10%: 75 New Hires by May 1

Compelling Lead

While the headline grabs attention and sometimes conveys news (as in the previous headline example), the lead (that is, the first paragraph) summarizes the primary news. Compare these two leads:

> **Lead 1:** A new, state-of-the-art database management software program is now available from ZXX, according to an announcement made today. The software uses revolutionary data-mining technology developed after years of research by ZXX's R&D team. The software, developed to meet the needs of small businesses, permits the tracking of leads five times faster than previous packages.
>
> **Lead 2:** ZXX's new database management software enables small businesses to track leads five times faster than previous packages.

That first lead uses clichés like *state-of-the-art* and *revolutionary*—turnoffs to editors, and even to consumers tired of reading fluff. Plus, the most important news—faster lead tracking—isn't mentioned until the third sentence. By that time, most editors, producers, and bloggers have moved on to the next release.

The second lead gets to the point much faster. In one sentence, it explains the software's benefit to small businesses—without over-the-top language.

Well-Organized Body

The body of the press release should build on the message in the headline and led. Using the example of ZXX, the next few paragraphs would explain why the software was developed, how it works, and how other small businesses have used it successfully.

A quote from the CEO or spokesperson offers a personal touch to the release and adds key information. Avoid quotes that simply repeat what's already been stated or that talk about the company's excitement, such as, "We're thrilled to offer this new product." Nobody cares! Instead, use quotes to further your message, such as by additional explanations of how the product benefits users.

Today, the format of a release can vary significantly; some have less text and include a list of links to images, videos, and key landing pages. Plus, some releases are further shortened to fit into a particular social media channel. Example B-6, a press release from a developer of a nutrition app, includes links to its website and logo.

EXAMPLE B-6
PRESS RELEASE ON INRFOOD NUTRITION APP

INRFOOD Offers More Personalized Nutrition With New Free Mobile App

TROPHY CLUB, Texas–INRFOOD (www.inrfood.com) has launched a free, customizable mobile app that gives people control over their nutrition, using information on what goes into their food and how diet affects their health. The app features an assortment of practical tools including calorie counting and ingredient analysis.

Founder and CEO Don O'Brien believes everyone deserves to know what's in their food. "Our motto is 'Trust What You Eat,' but that's difficult because the industrialized food system is more chemistry than biology, and many products have numerous additives. INRFOOD is spurring a grassroots nutrition revolution that's calling for more transparency in foods and ingredients."

Dietary guidance too often focuses on calories or carbs to the exclusion of micronutrients and other ingredients that are just as, if not more, important.

The headline incorporates the new app and the broader personalized nutrition story to intrigue journalists.

A concise lead expands on the headline's personalized nutrition message and explains the app's benefits.

The CEO's quote advances the story, discussing the movement toward transparency with ingredients.

The INRFOOD app makes deciphering these variables tremendously simple, bringing transparency to a complex topic.

The app's foundation is a growing database of more than 750,000 foods and 15,000 ingredients. Unlike one-size-fits-all nutrition labels, the app creates unique labels based on individual preferences: An endurance athlete and an office worker will obviously have different needs. Simple color coding and personalized alerts based on specific ingredients are further examples of the app adapting to the user, rather than the other way around.

The chance to discover delicious, healthy food and meal ideas is another key benefit of the app. It lets users see what others with similar nutrition profiles have been eating.

The INRFOOD app has been two years in the making. The development team's vision is a nutrition solution for every scenario—athletes, pregnant women, vegetarians, vegans, and so on. In the coming months, the team will be announcing new features and tools to bring this vision closer to reality.

O'Brien concluded, "To bring change to the food system, we need to empower people to make better food choices. A change in demand will accelerate this new food revolution. We plan on being the bridge to connect our community with all the best food choices available. Together with the user community, we can revolutionize our food and in turn, change everyone's lives for the better."

The app is available in the iTunes store. Visit www.inrfood.com for more info.

About INRFOOD

INRFOOD transforms lives with complete health and wellness in mind. It simplifies the complexities of nutrition with personalized alerts and recommendations. Instead of just counting calories, its app focuses on a

The last five paragraphs offer additional relevant information about the app and its potential impact. They're followed by another link to the company website and to the iTunes app store.

bottom-up approach through analysis of food's core components—its ingredients. The goal is to empower consumers to make better-informed dietary decisions specifically for their needs.

Contact:
Don O'Brien, CEO
573.873.6631
dobrien@inrfood.com

Press release used with permission of INRFOOD.

LinkedIn Profile Summary

Whether you're a business owner, consultant, executive, elected official, or job searcher, your LinkedIn profile is your most important personal branding tool. You can showcase your talents, accomplishments, connections, business philosophy, and more. And you can express your personality and tell your story, so prospects, employers, partners, and others will view you as the "right fit."

Search online and you'll find advice galore on how to create a "killer LinkedIn profile," much of which doesn't fit your requirements or style. At the same time, you can also find many prudent suggestions for incorporating key images and videos, featuring successful projects, highlighting relevant testimonials, referencing your LinkedIn groups, optimizing for mobile users, and more. For this discussion, we'll stick to strategies for writing your heading and summary—what readers see first.

While you can take many different approaches to creating an effective LinkedIn profile, your text should adhere to a few key principles that will increase the likelihood of connecting with the right person or organization.

Clarify Audience, Purpose, and Strategy

Be clear about who you're targeting, for what purpose, and the most pertinent message to attract attention. For example, if you're an internal auditor looking for a position at a large organization, your strategy might be to highlight your accomplishments, such as developing a cost-effective audit report process at a major corporation.

Craft Captivating Headings

Entice your target audience with a heading that immediately conveys your value and intrigues readers to find out what you can offer. Consider using multiple headings separated by one or more vertical bars (|). See these examples of engaging headings:

> PMP-certified project manager who has led multimillion-dollar projects worldwide.

After realizing I couldn't act for a living, I set the stage for hundreds of high-achieving businesswomen.

Don't Be Afraid to "Let Go"

Unlike a résumé, with limited space and common standards to follow, a LinkedIn profile allows you to be unconventional in your content and style—as long as you keep it professional. You could recap your work history with a humorous overtone. Or you could tell the story about an unusual event or circumstance that transformed your career. You could even use a whacky analogy to bring attention to your skills or to explain your strategy for solving a business problem.

Be sure that your content and linguistic devices relate to your core message, as in this heading: *Copywriter who crafts web content that goes viral. And you won't beat me at Scrabble!* The reference to Scrabble is ideal for a copywriter, who wants to be viewed as a wordsmith.

For some of you, this let-your-hair-down approach won't be appropriate. Maybe you work in a traditional industry like law, banking, or insurance. Or you're more comfortable talking about yourself in a straightforward manner. Whatever style you use, draw readers in with a compelling narrative. This could include an in-depth explanation of how your initiatives produced meaningful results, how you empowered direct reports to enhance their performance, or your thoughts on a particular industry issue.

Make Your Summary Compelling and Substantive

Whether you use a conventional or offbeat approach, your LinkedIn summary needs a powerful and substantive message that encourages your target audiences to connect with you. Build on the message in your heading. For example, as a human resource executive, your heading may read, *Helping international companies optimize employee performance.* Then your summary could offer examples of initiatives in which you maximized performance, ideally with metrics. You could also incorporate a story of how you resolved a difficult problem involving individuals from different countries whose cultures had clashed. Plus, you could cite a flattering testimonial from a C-suite executive.

Consider your LinkedIn profile summary as an extended elevator speech—which doesn't need to be rushed through in 60 seconds like at a networking event. Use this section to communicate your most important assets and your beliefs about your profession or industry. Although your text can go on and on, write summaries that are explicit and concise (see Step 2) to hold readers' attention. And recognize that many people won't bother reading any more of your profile.

See Example B-7, in which a marketing agency owner entices readers with an intriguing heading, followed by an offbeat presentation of her story, a synopsis of her experience and talents, and her approach to servicing clients.

EXAMPLE B-7
LINKEDIN PROFILE SUMMARY

Anne Marie (Kerr) Holder

Heading conveys her broad expertise, including the ability to optimize client expectations.

CEO/Client Expectations Optimizer + Brand Strategist + Advertising Agency Owner + PR Professional + Marketing Expert
SPARK Strategic Ideas
UNC Kenan-Flagler Business School

Her story, told in the third person with staccato sentences, reveals a bit about Anne Marie's personality and style, enticing the reader to learn more.

"Girl spends 10 years in big ad agencies. Earns her badges. Inhales a lot of smoke. So, she takes to the hills (Chapel Hill) and comes down knowing there is a smarter way to build it. With better tools, she sees the value in a lighter backpack. Fresh kindling. Same passion. And so it began. SPARK. Then she became we, and grew to a troop. Strategic. Agile. Smart cookies."

That's the fun way the SPARK website (sparksi.com) describes my journey. I got my start working for Charlotte ad agencies, working up to managing a $13 million account. Eventually, I realized that I had built a strong set of skills around advertising, public relations, and marketing, but I also recognized I had a lot of questions about the broader business world.

My hunger for knowledge felt limited in the agency environment so I set off to discover more about the business world and myself.

While working full time, I spent almost two years in an intensive executive MBA weekend program at the Kenan-Flagler School of Business. The program changed my very essence–teaching me to ask different questions, view things from all angles, and challenge assumptions. As it turned out, I have a talent for business strategy and really enjoy being able to combine strategic business planning with communications. I also knew there was a way to improve the traditional agency model, introduce transparency, and create an environment that nurtured employees with stronger results for our clients.

In 2008, I got the courage to ignite my passion and launch SPARK Strategic Ideas. It's been a wild ride, but it is incredibly gratifying to come to work every day, surrounded by a family of employees who love what they do and to know that every day, we make a difference. We are great at growing businesses. And when we grow a business, that business can hire more people. That changes lives. And in some small way, we change the world. Sometimes, it only takes a SPARK.

The last three paragraphs build on the charming opening, taking us through Anne Marie's steps to create a successful agency, culminating with a clever play on words with the company name.

LinkedIn profile summary used with permission of Anne Marie Holder.

Appendix C
Commonly Misused Words and Phrases

Accept, Except
- Accept means "to agree to," "to acknowledge," or "to tolerate": *She accepts your offer.*
- Except is typically a preposition that specifies what's excluded: *Each report was delivered on time except last quarter's sales analysis.*

Advice, Advise
- Advice is a recommendation for a certain action: *Fang's advice helped me complete the project faster.*
- Advise is "to inform" or "to notify": *We advise new hires to study the company's mission statement.*

Aggravate, Irritate
- Aggravate means "to worsen": *Al's frequent lateness aggravated the tension among his colleagues.*
- Irritate means "to annoy": *Mary's attitude irritated the |senior staff.*

All ready, Already
- All ready means that everybody or everything is ready: *After three rounds of edits, the activity report was all ready for the supervisor's review.*
- Already refers to something that occurred previously: *By the end of the second quarter, the marketing budget was already spent.*

Among, Between

- Among is used when referring to three or more items: *The CEO expects cooperation among the 12 departments.*
- Between is used when referring to two items: *He tried unsuccessfully to mediate the conflict between the two managers.*

Amount, Number

- Amount is used when referring to something that can't be counted: *The amount of space for the conference was hardly adequate.*
- Number is used when referring to items that can be counted: *Given the high number of client complaints, we need to improve our procedures.*

Any one, Anyone

- Any one refers to any single member of a group of people or items: *Any one of you could be promoted next quarter.*
- Anyone refers to any individual, but not to a particular person or group: *The company provides laptops to anyone who works at home.*

Bad, Badly

- Bad is an adjective (modifying a noun): *I hope that bad weather doesn't hurt attendance at the quarterly meeting.*
- Badly is an adverb (modifying a verb): *The client's receptionist was coughing badly.*

Bring, Take

- Bring is used for what's coming to your location: *The brand manager asked the account executive to bring the social media report to the meeting.*
- Take is used for what's being moved to where you're going: *Take the iPad on your trip to Houston.*

Compliment, Complement

- Compliment as a noun refers to a flattering remark or best wishes. As a verb, it means "to praise": *The CEO complimented Meg's outstanding leadership.*
- Complement, as a noun and verb, refers to an added feature that enhances something or goes well with it: *Paul's attention to detail complements his supervisor's big-picture thinking.*

Compose, Composed, Comprise

- Compose is "to produce": *Jean asked Alex to compose a history of the firm.*
- Composed means "made up": *The anthology is composed of five volumes.*
- Comprise means "consists of": *Canada comprises 10 provinces. (The phrase "comprised of" is never acceptable.)*

Device, Devise

- Device is an instrument or object designed for a specific purpose: *Sanjay ordered a special device to hold up the screen.*
- Devise is typically a verb that means "to plan" or "to invent": *Larry devised a plan to promote the firm's latest electronic gadgets.*

Discreet, Discrete

- Discreet refers to not attracting attention: *During the seminar, Tim made a discreet exit to the lobby to answer a call.*
- Discrete means "separate" or "distinct": *Internal communications and public relations are two discrete departments.*

Elicit, Illicit

- Elicit means "to provoke an action" or "to draw out something hidden": *Norah tried to elicit comments from the team about her web analytics report.*
- Illicit means "illegal": *The IT manager asked all employees to scan their computers weekly for illicit activity.*

Ensure, Insure

- Ensure is "to make something certain": *Please ensure that your expense reports are completed by the last day of the month.*
- Insure is "to be covered by an insurance policy" or "to protect against risk": *Small business owners should insure their companies against theft and fire.*

Explicit, Implicit

- Explicit means "clear" or "definite": *The instructions were explicit in requiring approval from the CFO before moving on to the next phase.*
- Implicit refers to something that was not stated but under-

stood: *Implicit in the email was the importance of getting feedback from employees at all levels.*

Fewer, Less

- Fewer is used for items that can be counted: *He took 10 fewer trips this year.*
- Less is used for something that can't be counted: *Since she was promoted to senior partner, Candice has spent less time with her direct reports.*

Good, Well

- Good is an adjective (modifying a noun): *Her presentation wasn't good.*
- Well is typically an adverb (modifying a verb): *The account manager did not perform well in the client meeting.*

Imply, Infer

- Imply is used when a speaker or writer indirectly suggests something: *In her presentation, Lauren implied that our chance for a bonus would depend on the company's net profits.*
- Infer is used by a listener or reader who determines what the speaker or writer meant but didn't say: *During Lauren's presentation, I inferred that our chance for a bonus would depend on the company's net profits.*

In to, Into

- In to can be used as a verb phrase (among other uses): *Lee came back in to remind Bob about his conference call.*
- Into indicates direction and movement: *The chief marketing officer walked into the room about 15 minutes late.*

It's, Its

- It's is the contraction for "it is" or "it has": *It's time to submit the proposal to YT Partners.*
- Its is a possessive pronoun that means "belonging to it": *The industry has always respected YC Industries and its senior executives.*

Lose, Loose

- Lose means "to misplace" or "to have something taken away": *If you don't respond promptly to clients' emails, you'll lose their respect.*

- Loose means "not tight-fitting" or "imprecise": *I was surprised that this year's regulations were so loose.*

May Be, Maybe

- May be refers to a possibility: *They may be late for the conference call.*
- Maybe, an adverb, means "possibly": *Maybe Steve can approve our budget by Friday.*

Precede, Proceed

- Precede means "come before": *The project conception phase always precedes the project planning phase.*
- Proceed means "to begin action": *After Amira emails her approval, proceed with the first step of the audit.*

Respectfully, Respectively

- Respectfully, an adverb (modifying a verb), means "showing respect": *Mike said he respectfully declined the invitation.*
- Respectively means "correspondingly," matching one item with another in the order given: *The laptop computer and laser printer cost about $900 and $400, respectively.*

Slow, Slowly

- Slow is an adjective (modifying a noun): *The annual meeting is always slow to get going.*
- Slowly is an adverb (modifying a verb): *To ensure the assistants understood their responsibilities, Linda spoke slowly during her presentation.*

Than, Then

- Than refers to a comparison: *The presentation ran 45 minutes longer than expected.*
- Then means "after that": *First review the specifications, and then proofread the report.*

That, Which

- That starts a restrictive clause whose absence would change the meaning of the sentence: *The* Wall Street Journal *is one newspaper that all our managers should read every morning.*
- Which starts a nonrestrictive clause, something that can be omitted without changing the meaning of the sentence:

The Wall Street Journal, *which covers many aspects of business, is extremely well written.*

Their, There, They're

- Their means "belonging to them": *Their performance was outstanding.*
- There means "in that place, "at that point," or "on that matter": *She explained that there are several options for solving the problem.*
- They're is the contraction for "they are": *They're always on time for meetings and conference calls.*

Your, You're

- Your means "belonging or relating to somebody": *Your most important job is to mentor new employees.*
- You're is the contraction for "you are": *I appreciate that you're always the first person to submit monthly expenses.*

Whose, Who's

- Whose is the possessive form of "who or which": *Simone is an example of a woman whose career advanced rapidly after her first promotion.*
- Who's is a contraction for "who is" or "who has": *Please email me the name of the new manager who's attending today's meeting.*

References

Bambu. 2017. *Q1 2017: Essential Data to Launch Your Employee Engagement & Advocacy Strategy.* Chicago: Bambu. https://getbambu.com/data-reports/engagement-to-advocacy.

Bernoff, J. 2016. "Bad Writing Costs Businesses Billions." *Daily Beast,* October 16. www.thedailybeast.com/bad-writing-costs-businesses-billions.

Dahl, G. 2007. *Advertising for Dummies,* 2nd Edition. Hoboken, NJ: Wiley Publishing.

Grossman, D. 2011. "The Cost of Poor Communications." *The Holmes Report,* July 16. www.holmesreport.com/latest/article/the-cost-of-poor-communications.

James, G. 2015. "New Study: The Average Worker Spends 30 Hours a Week Checking Email." *Inc.,* August 27. www.inc.com/geoffrey-james/new-study-the-average-worker-spends-30-hours-a-week-checking-email.html.

Killeen, J. 2013. "Poor Writing Skills Lead to Lost Business and Career Paralysis." *Los Angeles Business Journal* (Advertising Supplement), March 25. www.nsaglac.org/blog/wp-content/uploads/2013/06/LABJ-Exec-Education_1303.pdf.

Kwoh, L. 2012. "The Buzzwords We Can't Help Using." *Wall Street Journal,* May 23. https://blogs.wsj.com/atwork/2012/05/23/the-buzzwords-we-cant-help-using.

Lewkowicz, K. 2016. "April Email Market Share: Mobile Rises to 56%, Its Highest Point Yet." Litmus blog, May 10. https://litmus.com/blog/mobile-rises-to-56-market-share-longest-sustained-growth-in-2016.

Mark, G.J., S. Voida, and A.V. Cardello. 2012. "'A Pace Not Dictated by Electrons': An Empirical Study of Work Without Email." *Proceedings of the SIGCHI Conference on Human Factors in Computing Systems, 555-564.* Austin, TX: Association for Computing Machinery.

Mattice Zundel, C. 2017. " Increase employee professionalism in 30 mins." LinkedIn Pulse, March 20. www.linkedin.com/pulse/increase-employee-professionalism-30-mins-catherine.

National Commission on Writing and CollegeBoard. 2004. *Writing: A Ticket to Work. . . or a Ticket Out: A Survey of Business Leaders.* New York. www.collegeboard.com/prod_downloads/writingcom/writing-ticket-to-work.pdf.

Radicati Group. 2015. "Email Statistics Report, 2015-2019." Palo Alto, CA: Radicati Group. www.radicati.com/wp/wp-content/uploads/2015/02/Email-Statistics-Report-2015-2019-Executive-Summary.pdf.

Song, M., V. Halsey, and T. Burress. 2007. *The Hamster Revolution: How to Manage Your Email Before It Manages You.* San Francisco: Berret-Koehler.

About the Author

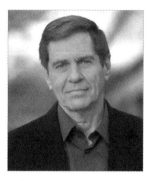

Jack Appleman, APR, CBC, is a prominent writing instructor, coach, and author who is committed to helping individuals achieve better results with their writing. He is driven by the belief that everyone can significantly improve their text by following a series of straightforward steps. Jack's workshops, webinars, and coaching sessions have helped thousands of working professionals become more confident and proficient writers.

As principal of the Monroe, New York–based Successful Business Writing, Jack brings more than 25 years' experience as a corporate trainer, professor, and public relations professional. He is a frequent speaker and has published several articles on the importance of good writing. He's also contributed to several articles in the *Wall Street Journal*. In 2015, Jack received the Charles T. Morgan Award for lifetime excellence in corporate training from the Association for Talent Development's Northern New Jersey chapter.

A professor since 2001, Jack teaches technical writing at Southern New Hampshire University. He received the accreditation in public relations certification from the Public Relations Society of America and the Certified Business Communicator designation from the Business Marketing Association. Jack also has a BA in communication from Ohio State University and an MS in journalism from Ohio University. He is studying for a PhD in organizational communication at the State University of New York at Albany. He can be reached on Twitter @writecoachJack and by email: jack@successfulbusinesswriting.com.

Index

G

getting started writing
  freewriting, 13–16, 120
  initial questions to answer, 9–10
  outlining complex documents, 12–13
  structured process, 16
  writing like you speak, 10–12

good business writing
  10 steps listed, 6–8
  demand for, 3
  payoff of, 5

grammar
  in emails, 148–149
  importance of, 101–102
  punctuation, 107
  rules
    dangling participles, 112–113
    pronoun-noun agreement, 107–109
    putting phrases in the correct positions, 113–114
    subject-verb agreement, 109–110
    tenses, 110
    using "and" to clarify connections, 113
    writing complete sentences, 111–112
  rules that can be broken, 114–115
  verbs, 36–38
  word usage errors, 115–116, 207–212

H

headlines
  for press releases, 197–198
  for social media, 159

I

improving writing within your organization
  cultivating a writing culture, 172–175
  designing a training course, 168–172
  developing a style guide, 173–174
  getting management buy-in, 167–168
  identifying individuals who need help, 166–167
  upgrading your own writing skills, 174
  writing-outcomes link, 165–166
information overload, 73

L

language. *See also* tone
  avoiding arrogance, 82
  compelling words, 74–76
  saying "no" tactfully, 89–90
  softening the impact of your message, 86–87
  word usage errors, 115–116, 207–212
learning how to be an effective writer, 4–5
LinkedIn, 162, 202–205
lists
  bulleted, 40–41, 60
  framing, 61–62
  numbered, 59–60
  subcategories for, 60–61

M

managerial method of organization, 62–63
mechanics, reviewing the, 124–125
message
  customizing the, 78–80
  editing and clarifying the, 25–26, 122
misunderstandings, avoiding
  comma usage, 103–104
  improving comprehension, 2
  putting phrases in the correct positions, 113–114
  unrelated ideas in one sentence, 47

O

organization
  bulleted lists, 40–41, 59–62
  creating a cohesive document, 51–52
  editing to evaluate, 123–124
  methods
    by comparison, 66
    by existing categories, 68
    by problem and solution, 67–68
    by order of importance, 63–64
    by space, 66
    by time, 65–66
    managerial, 62–63
    selecting the appropriate, 68–69
  separating ideas into chunks, 54–56
  starting with the bottom line, 52–54
  using subheads to increase readability, 56–59
  visual appeal, 69–71
outlining complex documents, 12–13, 123